UNITED STATES FOREIGN AID:

Readings in the Problem Area of Wealth

Date Due

JA 18 '61			
MY 22 '61			
MY 12 '62			
AP 24 '64			
MY 17 '66			
DE 16 '66			
JA 31 '67			
MR 5 '68			
MY 23 '69			
MAR 1 3 1978			
FEB 1 3 1985			
FEB 1 1 1993			

CHANDLER STUDIES IN
INTERNATIONAL AND
INTERCULTURAL
RELATIONS

Nationalism and International Progress
Compiled and Edited by
URBAN G. WHITAKER, JR.

Nuclear Weapons, Missiles, and Future War:
Problem for the Sixties
Compiled and Edited by
CHARLES A. McCLELLAND

Propaganda and International Relations
Compiled and Edited by
URBAN G. WHITAKER, JR.

The Underdeveloped Lands:
A Dilemma of the International Economy
Compiled and Edited by
DeVERE E. PENTONY

United States Foreign Aid:
Readings in the Problem Area of Wealth
Compiled and Edited by
DeVERE E. PENTONY

The United Nations:
The Continuing Debate
Compiled and Edited by
CHARLES A. McCLELLAND

UNITED STATES FOREIGN AID

Readings in the Problem Area of Wealth

Compiled and Edited by
DeVERE E. PENTONY
San Francisco State College

With the Assistance of
MORLEY SEGAL AND MARILYN DERICHS

HOWARD CHANDLER, PUBLISHER
660 MARKET STREET
SAN FRANCISCO 4, CALIFORNIA

Preface to the Series

The series of readings of which this volume is one part stems from a prolonged practical experiment in the teaching of international relations. In the time since the origin of the academic field of international relations at the close of World War I, the question of what should be done in the introductory course has never been resolved to the satisfaction of a majority of college teachers and students but, on the other hand, the interest in how the course ought to be organized and what it should include has never flagged. The pluralistic character of American higher education makes certain that no flat uniformity in the college curriculum will prevail. In a truly unique fashion, each American institution arrives at its own choices of how it will meet the two basic responsibilities of the higher learning—the transmission of what is known and the exploration of what remains in mystery.

At San Francisco State College, faculty deliberations between 1946 and 1948 led to the creation of a new core curriculum in the lower division. One of the courses of study that the faculty brought into being was a broadly conceived and basic study of the international environment of the twentieth-century world. Almost a decade of trial and error with this course confirmed two hypotheses: (1) The teaching of the principles and processes of international behavior is a part of liberal education that college students appreciate for its importance to their understanding. (2) It is extremely difficult to construct a coherent and significant course of study that will meet the standards of the academic disciplines of the social sciences.

A generous grant from the Carnegie Corporation of New York made it possible to launch in 1958 a number of studies and experiments concerned with the undergraduate teaching and study of international relations. These studies and experiments are at midpoint at the time of this writing. They include a testing program of the ideas, attitudes, knowledge, and learning progress of undergraduate college students in international relations, a comparison of the effectiveness of two different approaches to the basic course (as the "transformation course" and as the "area course"), an experiment in high-school instruction in world affairs, some trials of gaming and simulation as undergraduate teaching auxiliaries, and a survey of the organization and content of the undergraduate-major patterns in international relations.

The collections of readings that appear in this series were first assembled with little thought of general publication. The staff of the San Francisco International Studies Project found that it needed to put in the hands of students in the experimental sections of the basic course some reading materials of a kind not found in the textbooks or in other collections of readings. Some twelve hundred pages, organized under ten topical headings, were brought together and used for a year in the "transformation course." Revisions were carried through during the summer of 1959.

It should not be supposed that this series reflects the full conception of the experimental course as it is being taught. Only a few of the more successful sets of readings appear in the series. Further, each of the collections was designed to illustrate through cases, problems, and issues some main aspect of drastic change or transformation going on in the international environment of the immediate past and present. Of course, one does not grasp the nature or significance of drastic changes in the conditions of international relations without a knowledge of what has gone before and of the attributes and characteristics of past practice and previous organization. We have supplied this necessary description of the past by means of classroom lectures and assignments in the standard textbooks and other reading. This series of readings carries, however, the main burden of introducing the changeful, novel, uncertain, and controversial elements of the situation.

The full theme of "transformation" might be set forth as follows: "In the system of relationships among nations, including interpersonal, intergroup, interorganizational, and intergovernmental aspects, what are the influences and forces that are impelling rapid and fundamental changes? If the relatively stable arrangements of the international affairs of the nineteenth-century world are taken as reference, what do we find of significance in the emerging international system of the late twentieth century?" Thus, the multiple revolutions in the military technology, in national organization, in communications, and in economic-ecological conditions become of central interest in the setting of how international relationships used to be maintained and how they appear to be taking on new forms and new functions.

It is the experience of the San Francisco International Studies group that the transformation theme can be developed in several different ways and in a number of conceptual perspectives. However the job is done, we have found at first hand that college students, once they have grasped the general idea, become eager to read, learn, and discuss its specific aspects and its broad implications. It is the hope of the compilers of these readings that they will be found useful to other college teachers and students. We venture the further suggestion that, in light of the many overlappings of subject matter and meaning in the social sciences and the humanities, one or several of these volumes may have value for courses that do not bear the formal label of international relations.

Charles A. McClelland
DeVere E. Pentony
Urban G. Whitaker, Jr.

October, 1959

Acknowledgments

This book of readings was made possible by funds granted by the Carnegie Corporation of New York. That Corporation is not, however, the author, owner, publisher, or proprietor of this publication and is not to be understood as approving by virtue of its grant any of the statements or views expressed herein.

The editor is grateful to the following publishers and publications for granting permission to reprint materials for which they hold copyright: *The American Assembly, American Mercury, The Annals of the American Academy of Political and Social Sciences, Committee for Economic Development, The New Republic, The Virginia Quarterly Review, The Wall Street Journal,* and *The Yale Review*.

This work was greatly aided by the secretarial assistance of Miss Merrit Cross of the San Francisco International Studies Project. It would hardly have been possible without the untiring efforts of Miss Marilyn Derichs and Morley Segal, who searched long and hard for appropriate material and performed valuable additional services of criticism and advice.

DeVere E. Pentony

San Francisco
October 2, 1959

Contents

I

Introduction

Few problems facing the American people and the American government are as filled with emotion, half-truth, misunderstandings, ignorance, and confusion as is the problem of American foreign-aid policy. Yet few problems may have such immediate *and* long-range importance for the United States, for on the solution of this problem may depend in some degree the economic viability, stability, and strength of the United States, the world, and the consumer dollar. And the whole program is enmeshed in the question of the place of the United States in a changing political, economic, and cultural world. The enormity of the problem can be indicated by the fact that since the end of World War II the United States has spent more than 70 billion dollars on foreign aid—an amount approximately equal to the total assessed property valuation of thirteen American cities (New York, Chicago, San Francisco, among others). If we are staggered by the fact that Americans spend some five billion dollars per year on candy and chewing gum, then surely this foreign-aid expenditure confounds and overawes the imagination.

Once we realize the amount of money spent, a torrent of questions may spring to mind. Some of the questions seem simple: What are the objectives of our foreign-aid programs? What have been the results? Where should the aid go? How should it be administered? Why should we aid anybody? Why not trade instead of aid? Although these questions seem relatively straightforward and uninvolved, they are highly complex and perplexing.

The problems raised by such questions command the attention and the concerted effort of some of the best minds in the world. They baffle and disturb the legislator, the administrator, the public, and the expert; they challenge the economist, the social scientist, and the politician. The complexity is easily demonstrated by developing any one of the above questions into a series of other questions. For example, the question of what are the objectives of the foreign-aid programs leads into questions like this: Are the objectives primarily to promote the security of the United States? Or are they humanitarian objectives? Or are they primarily to promote our own economic interests? Or are they all three? If the objective is security, how is security to be defined? Does it mean that our aid should be primarily in the form of military aid to our allies? Or must we give them economic aid so that they can afford a bigger defense program of their own? Conversely, can our security interests be defined so broadly as to justify giving aid to the neutralist countries of the world on the grounds of promoting our security? Or again, does the concern over security argue that we should reduce our foreign aid and spend the money on weapons and the training of men that we can trust in the event of a challenge to that security?

If the objective is humanitarian, aren't we misplacing the emphasis? Shouldn't we cut the military aid and spend that money for nonmilitary goods and services? Or should we aid famine-stricken areas in Red China?

If the objective is the promotion of the American economy, should we channel more of our aid into areas from which we will get maximum economic returns? Or perhaps we could do more for our economy by spending the money at home on roads, schools, hospitals. These questions and many more are raised by the one question of what the objectives of the program are. Small wonder that foreign aid is a complicated problem, when even the questions (let alone the answers) are so involved. However, it is hoped that the reader will be able to make some sense out of the complexity and arrive at some answers that are reasonable, logical, and realistic. At the very least, he may realize that many of the issues are not black and white, but frequently shadings of gray.

The readings that we have chosen range broadly both in quality and quantity. They include material that one might see in the paper, hear on the radio or television, or read in the scholarly journals and the news magazines. This is not to say that the subject does not have its comic and ludicrous aspects. As part of the human comedy it is bound to, and we have included a reading or two in that vein. But perhaps the serious side will be grasped and will lead to the realization that we are all involved with the problem of foreign aid in one way or another.

The reader will also find, as he reads and listens, that charge and countercharge by opponents and proponents mount to a crescendo of dissonance, suspicion, and confusion that make the subject seem the twentieth-century counterpart to the tower of Babel. In this, the age of the sloganeer, many of us are probably familiar with some of the taunts and righteous defenses of foreign aid. To refresh our memory here are a few:

"Foreign aid is bleeding America white." "It is a necessary link in the chain of American prosperity." "It is money down a rathole." "It is vital to American security in a war-prone world." "It is money out of the pockets of hardworking Americans who consequently fall ever more deeply into the arms of the tax collector." "It's a colossal, gigantic giveaway." "It is a shrewd, self-serving policy grounded in the American national interest." "It's a Wall Street plan to enslave the world." "It's a Christian plan to save the world." "It's a conspiracy of certain big financiers to enhance their profit position." "It's just another case of naive Uncle Sam assuming his international role of Uncle Stupid." "It's poorly planned, poorly administered, and poorly thought out." "It is the product of the most intensively, extensively and thoroughly discussed policy in the history of the United States." "It is engendered by a self-perpetuating bureaucracy that has been continually unsure and confused as to its purposes, its methods, and its possible results." "It is based on solid investigation, private and public, expert and lay, as to its objectives, successes and failures, and its administration." "It is dollar diplomacy, colonialism of the worst sort." "It is international togetherness, sharing." "It is the frantic dying gasp of a decadent capitalist society." "It is a remarkable demonstration of the vitality of the capitalist system." "It's a threat to the solvency of the American economy, to the life of the American businessman." "It's a way of supplying raw materials for the voracious American industrial machine." "It's giving the American largesse to foreigners when it can better be used for our own poor, weak and dissatisfied." "It's building up our stockpiles and our sources of supply so that we can supply our industrial machine when our resources are no longer so plentiful." "It means inflation." "It means more jobs."

These are some of the charges, claims, and contentions focused on foreign aid. Not all of them will be answered in this series of readings, but many of them will. Some of them are reasonable. Some are not. Some of the claims both for and against cannot be maintained in the face of searching analysis and concrete facts. Others are truly matters of opinion, where one educated guess as to the proper alternative may be as good as another. It is part of the task of the reader to separate the rational from the irrational, the logical from the illogical, and to shape an informed opinion. In a sense, this is an adventure in critical analysis.

Moreover, it is hoped that insight will be gained into the fact that the world is a world of change and that the United States' position in that world is a changing one. There are several alternatives open, several paths to take, several decisions to make. The United States may be on the brink of disaster or it may be at the beginning of a brave new world. Or perhaps all foreign policy, including foreign-aid policy, is destined to operate in a sea of half-truths and partial rationality, where the only practical alternative is muddling through. What the ultimate, long-run answers are no one may know, but we live in the short run and must comment on the perplexing human and natural events either by silence or action. Whatever the choice, there may be no easily identifiable rewards. The satisfaction may come only in the seeking.

II

The Background and Scope
of Foreign Aid

The readings begin with a short resumé of United States foreign-aid expenditures compiled by Herman F. Ficker. It indicates the tremendous monetary scope of the foreign-aid programs since 1940 and the general direction and form that the expenditures have taken.

The next article is an excerpt from a longer study prepared by The Center of International Studies of the Massachusetts Institute of Technology. Entitled "The Historical Background of United States Foreign Aid," it provides a brief historical survey of American activities in this area and thus sets the stage for many of the discussions that follow. It attempts to identify the objectives of American foreign-aid acivities in the past and the specific means for achieving these objectives. A pertinent question that arises from this article is whether the world situation has now changed so drastically that the "old" objectives and the "old" means for achieving them are still appropriate. Indeed, this question might be the question theme of this whole series of readings.

SOME STATISTICS ON
FOREIGN-AID EXPENDITURES*

HERMAN L. FICKER

HERMAN L. FICKER *is a member of the International Finance and Trade Unit of the Economic Division of the Library of Congress.*

During the period July 1, 1940, through June 30, 1958, the United States extended gross utilized aid totaling $120,775,799,000 to foreign governments and international organizations as follows:

War Period, July 1, 1940-June 30, 1945

Gross grants (Lend-lease)	$46,728,287,000
Gross grants (all other)	1,400,010,000
Utilized credits and loans	1,095,562,000
TOTAL	**$49,223,859,000**

Postwar Period, July 1, 1945-June 30, 1958

Gross grants	$55,017,837,000
Utilized credits and loans	16,534,103,000
TOTAL	**$71,551,940,000**

(Gross grants were reduced by $2,256,854,000 consisting of prior grants converted to credits. . . .)

Not included in the overall total of aid are U.S. capital investments of $3,420,000,000—in the International Bank, $635,000,000; International Monetary Fund $2,750,000,000; International Finance Corporation, $35,000,000.

Although these investments constitute an additional measure taken by the U.S. Government to promote foreign economic development, they do not result in immediate equivalent aid to foreign countries. . . .

* Reprinted from *U.S. Congressional Record*, 86th Congress, 1st Session, 1959, pp. A828-836.

AVAILABILITIES OF AID, JULY 1, 1958

Foreign grant and credit authorization available during fiscal year 1957 approximated $14.8 billions. Total utilizations during the year amounted to $5.4 billions in grants and credits. The Office of Business Economics of the U.S. Department of Commerce estimated that, as of July 1, 1958, foreign grants and credits available and still to be furnished from prior authorizations amount to approximately $9.5 billions. This did not mean that these carryover funds consisted of cash available for disbursement. These funds were substantially committed in long-range contracts under which goods and services had not yet been delivered. The availabilities by category comprised: Grants of military supplies and services, $3.4 billion; Other economic grants, $2.1 billion; Credits and loans, $3.9 billion.

In addition to these carryover funds, the 85th Congress, 2d session, provided $6.1 billion in new appropriations for foreign aid: Export-Import Bank Act, $2 billion; Mutual Security, $3.3 billion; Estimated available proceeds of additional sales under amendment to Agricultural Trade Development and Assistance Act, $.8 billion.

Thus the carryover funds of $9.5 billions plus new funds of $6.1 billions provided an estimated availability of $15.6 billions for foreign aid during fiscal year 1959.

This approximate total may be disbursed under the following three main categories:

Grants of military supplies and services, $4.9 billion; Other economic grants, $3.5 billion; Credits and loans, $7.1 billion.

POSTWAR MILITARY AID

The breakdown of military aid by country is not given as such information is classified for security reasons. Cumulative military disbursements during the postwar period are stated for the following regions:

Asia and the Pacific	$ 4,590,297,000
Europe	12,889,192,000
Near East, Africa and south Asia	2,740,317,000
Other areas and overlapping programs	225,440,000
TOTAL	$20,445,246,000

It should be clearly understood that any total for postwar aid by the United States to any foreign country compiled from these tables will consist of economic grants and loans only. Military totals will not be included so that final aid totals are only a partial representation of disbursements.

DEFINITIONS

Grants are transfers for which no repayment is generally expected, but might involve an obligation on the part of the receiver to extend aid to the United States or other countries to achieve a common objective.

Credits are loan disbursements or transfers under agreements for specific repayments over a period of years, usually with interest. In some instances aid has been given under grants with the understanding that a decision as to repayment would be made at a later date. When such a decision for repayment is made a credit is established. As a rule such credits are not deducted from the grants recorded in previous periods. Only after the agreement for repayment is signed, an adjustment is made from grants to credits.

Credits to individual countries may include loans to private entities; e.g., loans to Canada represent credits extended solely to private interests.

The measure of foreign grants and credits generally is in terms of goods delivered or shipped by the U.S. Government, services rendered by the U.S. Government, or cash disbursed by the U.S. Government to or for the account of a foreign government or entity.

Reverse grants and returns on grants comprise: (1) Reverse lend-lease received in the immediate postwar years; (2) the return of military equipment loans, usually aircraft and watercraft; (3) the return of civilian supplies; (4) the return of military naval ships as well as lend-lease merchant ships; (5) the cash war-account settlements for lend-lease and other grants; (6) and finally, the foreign currency funds resulting from military aid collections, usually for administrative expenses, as well as the counterpart funds resulting from economic and technical assistance.

At the end of the war period such reverse grants, reciprocal lend-lease, and returns on grants amounted to $7,872,637,000.

During the postwar period ending June 30, 1958, such returns totaled $1,805,343,000.

During [the total war and postwar periods], the United States authorized net credits and loans including conversions from prior grants for an aggregate of $20,481,987,000. On June 30, 1958 the unutilized total amounted to $2,692,682,000. This would be available as lines of credit to be drawn down during fiscal year 1959 or until such time as the authorizations expired.

Direct utilizations since 1940 amounted to $17,302,055,000 and an additional $487,250,000 were lent through agent banks by the Export-Import Bank.

Since 1945 such utilizations including reconversions have amounted to $16,534,103,000.

Repayments of loans or principal collected by the respective U.S. Government agencies on the credits extended, the loans, sales, commodity programs and prior grants converted into credits have amounted to $5,595,364,000 since 1940. The major portion, or $5,153,859,000, has been collected during the postwar period since 1945.

During fiscal year 1957 utilizations of credits amounted to $440,282,000 and collections were $639,574,000. This trend was reversed during fiscal year 1958 when utilizations totaled $1,226,736,000 and collections $614,769,000.

Outstanding on June 30, 1958, or utilizations unrepaid, amounted to $12,179,482,000. During the past 18 years principal charged off as uncollectible has amounted to less than one-tenth of 1 percent of the total lent or credit utilized.

Welfare data included under postwar grant aid comprise government grants of agricultural food surpluses distributed overseas by private American welfare agencies, churches or international agencies such as CARE. These agencies undertook the free distribution of such surpluses as part of their oversea missionary commitments.

[The area distribution of $71 billion of United States aid between July 1, 1945 and June 30, 1958 was approximately as follows:]

The American Republics received a total of $2.8 billion as follows:

	(In Millions)
Argentina	131
Bolivia	147
Brazil	794
Chile	198
Colombia	161
Costa Rica	38

Cuba	42
Dominican Republic	3
Ecuador	51
El Salvador	9
Guatemala	70
Haiti	48
Honduras	13
Mexico	414
Nicaragua	19
Panama	25
Paraguay	23
Peru	155
Uruguay	15
Venezuela	21
Inter-American Organizations	11
(Military and other unspecified by country	489)

② Europe received a total of $31.5 billion as follows:

	(In Millions)
Albania	20
Austria	1,139
Belgium-Luxembourg	823
Czechoslovakia	215
Denmark	304
Finland	144
France	6,876
East Germany	17
West Germany	5,207
Hungary	32
Iceland	43
Ireland	146
Italy (including Trieste)	3,240
Netherlands	1,353
Norway	379
Poland	463
Portugal	91
Spain	472
Sweden	111
Switzerland	2
USSR	688
U.K.	8,878
Yugoslavia	860

The Near East and South Asia received a total of $4.9 billion as follows:

(In Millions)

Afghanistan	64
Ceylon	22
Greece	1,907
India	617
Iran	366
Iraq	16
Israel	513
Jordan	73
Lebanon	28
Nepal	11
Pakistan	424
Saudi Arabia	23
Turkey	834
United Arab Republic	26

The Far East and Pacific received a total of 11.2 billion as follows:

(In Millions)

Australia	27
Burma	27
Cambodia	122
China-Taiwan	2,654
Indo-China	111
Indonesia	314
Japan	3,544
Korea	2,186
Laos	153
Malaya	1
New Zealand	19
Philippines	988
Thailand	130
Trust Territory of the Pacific	44
Vietnam	830

Africa received a total of $260 million as follows:

(In Millions)

Ethiopia	28
Ghana	.5

The United Nations and other International Organizations received a total of $1.4 billion.

THE HISTORICAL BACKGROUND OF UNITED STATES FOREIGN AID*

THE CENTER FOR INTERNATIONAL STUDIES
Massachusetts Institute of Technology

The Center for International Studies of the Massachusetts Institute of Technology was established in 1951 to sponsor and conduct research and research training in foreign policy and international relations.

INTRODUCTION

Our postwar aid programs are the heirs of lend-lease. From 1941 to 1945 we harnessed some $41 billion of our resources (net) to the clear military purpose of winning a major war, by making our allies more effective in the field than they would otherwise have been in opposing a coalition which sought to dominate the great Eurasian continent. Over the past 12 years our aid programs have been designed to support a number of different objectives of American foreign and military policy.

* Reprinted from "The Objectives of United States Economic Assistance Programs," U.S. Senate, The Special Committee to Study the Foreign Aid Program, *The Foreign Aid Program*, 85th Congress, 1st Session, 1957, Sec. I, pp. 4-15.

Roughly speaking, the programs of economic aid which succeeded lend-lease have passed through three major stages since the latter days of the Second World War: aid in relief and rehabilitation (1944-46); assistance in longer term reconstruction (1947-50); military aid and support (1951-56). As will become clear, these distinctions are not hard and fast: For example, significant military aid to Greece and Turkey was undertaken as early as 1947. But the three phases characterize the major directions of the American aid effort.

In addition, starting with the creation of the International Bank, there has been a continuing minor strand of long-run development assistance woven into the American aid programs.

The purpose of this section is to review briefly these phases and the role of long-run development assistance in American policy. The chapter concludes with an effort to identify the common larger purposes which appear to underlie the continuing support of the Congress for these substantial efforts, now maintained by the United States for more than a decade, and to define the central issue we confront in reshaping our aid policy.

SHORT-TERM RELIEF AND REHABILITATION

In the first instance the purpose of economic aid was simply to assist our wartime allies in finding their feet after a long, disruptive, and costly war. In joining in the agreement for United Nations Relief and Rehabilitation on November 9, 1943 the Nation expressed its determination—

> that immediately upon the liberation of any area by the armed forces of the United Nations or as a consequence of retreat of the enemy, the population thereof shall receive aid and relief from their sufferings, food, clothing and shelter, aid in the prevention of pestilence and in the recovery of the health of the people, and that preparation and arrangements shall be made for the return of prisoners and exiles to their homes and for assistance in the resumption of urgently needed agricultural and industrial production and the restoration of essential services. . . .

In addition to UNRRA operations, relief and rehabilitation were conducted by American military forces as one area after another was liberated. In a narrow sense such aid could be justified as a way of avoiding "disease and unrest" in regions of military occupation by American troops. Indeed, that was the formal basis for the initial aid programs in ex-enemy territories. But military assistance had, in fact, the same simple humanitarian foundations as the UNRRA program.

The initial postwar loan to Great Britain had essentially the same character. It was designed to tide the country over a transitional period during which time the economy of a key nation—and a deserving ally—would recover and restructure itself, without undergoing a fall in its standard of welfare, and then fit into the sort of world economy to which Americans looked forward.

In addition to these sources of transitional aid, a wide range of other forms of credits and grants were made available to help restore a disrupted world economy. Transitional aid granted in 1945-46 totaled about $8 billion. Why was it granted?

The executive branch of the Government, the Congress, and the American people as a whole in the period of 1944-45 had thrashed out a concept of the sort of postwar world they wanted. It was, essentially, a world in which the failures of 1919 and of the interwar years, as those failures were then understood, would not be repeated. As a nation we looked to an era of peace in which the security issues of the world would be handled by a United Nations, built, in turn, around the continued unity of the three major wartime allies. With this foundation we sought a prosperous, expanding world economy in which trade would become increasingly free, currencies would become convertible, and the productive possibilities of exchange among nations would be exploited without reference to narrowly national security policies.

It was in this mood of hope, aspiration, and good intentions that the International Bank and the International Monetary Fund were set up as a result of the Bretton Woods agreements, the convertibility clause was written into the British loan agreements, and the first moves were made to establish the International Trade Organization. Thus, also, America gave freely of its resources to cover what was expected to be the relatively brief gap in time between the abnormal world of the immediate postwar days and the emergence of the international system assumed in the setting up of the United Nations and its related institutions.

Americans were not unmindful of the danger that communism might spread in the period of postwar disruption. The memory of Communist efforts—successful and unsuccessful—to exploit the opportunities open after the First World War was still alive in the country and in the Congress in 1944-46. But, by and large, American aid was given in these years in a mood of hope rather than fear, as a means of converting a world torn by battle into a world organization for a productive peace.

In the course of 1946 it became increasingly clear that the assumptions underlying the wartime vision of the postwar world were, one by one, being rendered untenable. Stalin evidently decided that the opportunities for Communist expansion in Europe and elsewhere were very great, given the weaknesses of the non-Communist world and the rapid American demobilization, accompanied as it was by a turning inward to American domestic problems. In 1946 also the Chinese Communists came to perceive that it might be possible for them to move immediately toward the total control of China which had always been their objective. Day by day in the executive branch, the Congress, and in the minds of the American people it became increasingly evident that the wartime vision of world peace and order would not immediately come to pass and that the Nation faced a security challenge of the first order of magnitude.

In the spring of 1947 the whole approach of the United States toward foreign policy was radically altered, and with this revision foreign aid assumed a new role, entering its second postwar stage. This change was precipitated by the British inability to continue to support Greece, which was in a state of civil war, and Turkey, which was under a great deal of diplomatic pressure from the Soviet Union, including a military threat which required a state of mobilization the Turkish economy could not sustain with its own resources.

The situations in Greece and Turkey immediately posed a range of issues which were to lie at the heart of American foreign policy over the next decade. Assuming that we cared enough about the independence of Greece and Turkey to vote American taxpayer's money to support them—

1. How much aid was required to do the job?
2. How should that aid be divided between economic and military categories?
3. How should conflicts between immediate military and long-run economic aid programs be resolved?

The difficulty arose because Greece, and, to a lesser degree,

Turkey faced two threats from communism. One was the external threat, united in the Greek case with Communist-led military insurrection; the other was the threat of political and social disintegration caused in turn by economic stagnation exploitable by local Communists.

It was widely recognized in the United States that an emergency program for Greece and Turkey was an inadequate answer to the problem posed for the United States in the late winter of 1947. Indeed, President Truman's private briefing for Members of Congress on February 27 (preceding his speech of March 12 to both Houses of Congress) had embraced not merely Greece and Turkey but the whole European economic position and the threat of Soviet exploitation of its consequent political weaknesses. There was also a widespread sense that the Greek and Turkish aid agreements stressed too heavily the military countermeasures to communism and were not sufficiently constructive and economic. On June 5, 1947, with Secretary Marshall's speech, the character of the European economic and political problem was fully faced and the familiar sequence of events which launched the Marshall plan was set in motion.

Stalin immediately recognized that the Marshall plan was an effective counter to his plans and intentions in Western Europe. As Molotov left Paris in July he warned the West of Moscow's implacable opposition to the joint venture, and the Communists opened up promptly an ominous campaign of political propaganda in the West, accompanied by disruptive Communist Party tactics. In addition, Stalin moved to tighten up and consolidate his Eastern European empire. In February 1948 the coup d'état was executed in Prague; and, in the course of the spring, Tito openly defied Stalin's effort to impose absolute control on Yugoslavia, producing not merely a major defeat for Moscow but heightening tension between East and West generally. In Germany, where tension between the Soviet Union and the West also rose, it was climaxed by the Berlin blockade, successfully met by the American and allied airlift during the winter of 1948-49.

The early, decisive stage of the Marshall plan, when the European economy gathered momentum, was thus colored by an atmosphere of danger from the East. Europeans felt a profound sense of insecurity as they went about reconstruction with no significant protection against the Soviet divisions massed in Eastern Germany except the distant capability of the United States to counter Soviet ground forces with atomic attack. Freshly released from German occupation, Western Europeans did not find reassuring a position from which, once again, they might have to be rescued after invasion from the East. It was initially as a psychological measure—to give Western Europeans the confidence to proceed with the reconstruction of their societies—that a joint European military effort was launched, which was to lead on to NATO, SHAPE, and the third stage of American economic aid.

While the European recovery program proceeded forward in good order, from 1948 to June 1950, backed by some $12 billion in grants and loans over the 3-year period, large sums were thrown in also in an effort to aid Nationalist China in the final stages of the Chinese civil war and then to establish the Taiwan base, while Japan and Korea were helped toward political and economic stability on much the same grounds as Germany, Austria, and Italy. The Asian programs totaled almost $4 billion in the 5 years preceding the attack on South Korea.

MILITARY AID AND SUPPORT

It was, of course, the outbreak of the Korean war which transformed military aid from a minor to a major aspect of the American program. As noted earlier, military aid had begun in 1947 in Greece and Turkey, and military needs were a major rationale for aid to Nationalist China. Moreover, the Mutual Defense Assistance Act of 1949 had provided military aid in a number of directions, including relatively small amounts for Europe. But, by and large, the assumptions underlying American policy at this stage were that Stalin did not plan to use limited wars to advance his objectives; that a war was possible and required deterrence; but that, if Stalin launched a major war, the free world could rely primarily in the first instance on the American Strategic Air Command and its atomic weapons delivery capabilities.

This assumption began to be reexamined after the first Soviet atomic explosion in September 1949. In Europe the notion gradually spread that an atomic stalemate might develop in which it would be irrational for Europeans to rely solely on American atomic weapons delivery capabilities against the Soviet ground forces. Support slowly grew for a European ground forces establishment which might be capable of deterring Soviet aggression. On the whole, however, European recovery continued to have a clear-cut priority over European defense, and NATO moved to the center of the stage only after the outbreak of the Korean war at the end of June 1950.

By September 1950 the issue of German rearmament began gingerly to be faced and, as NATO grew and the United States moved to shore up free Asia, the proportion of military assistance within the total foreign-aid budget increased. Even then military assistance represented only 24 percent of foreign aid in the fiscal year 1951, 38 percent in 1952. In the Mutual Security Act of 1952, however, military assistance was more than two-thirds of the total authorization for fiscal 1953.

The underlying purpose of this program was simple and clear. It was to permit other nations to maintain sufficient military establishments to make unattractive to Moscow and Peking aggressive adventures similar to the Korean war; and in the case of Indochina—down to the Geneva Conference of 1954—to permit the French to continue to deal with the Vietminh threat. From the American point of view, the buildup of NATO and then of SEATO was a way of maintaining deterrence without engaging substantial American troop formations. This remained the fundamental rationale for the American aid programs, in their major dimension, down through 1956.

As the mutual aid program developed, it was recognized that the maintenance of these deterrent forces in the common interest constituted a substantial drain on the economies of the weaker states; and large programs of economic aid in the form of defense support accompanied the development of our military alliances in the period 1952-56, in which 5-year period some $24 billion was spent under the military security program.

In the course of these years, however, the underlying basis for the military aid programs developed after the outbreak of the Korean war was gradually altered and eroded by three major factors.

First, the Soviet Union developed substantial capabilities in atomic (including fusion) weapons, means of delivery, and means of defense. From the time of the first explosion of a Soviet fusion device in August 1953 the heart began to go out of NATO as a ground-force establishment. The conviction gradually grew that the capabilities of mutual destruction were now such that an all-out atomic war was wholly irrational unless 1 of the 2 major atomic powers achieved capabilities sufficient to knock out at a blow the other's retaliatory power; and that, in the context of a Soviet-American atomic standoff, a ground-force war would be impossible to fight in Europe without triggering an all-out war. The maintenance in the free world of an adequate degree of deterrence against atomic war was evidently a job primarily for the United States; and American secrecy regulations precluded effective European participation in the contribution to the deterrence of atomic war except insofar as Britain developed atomic weapon capabilities on its own.

The will of Europeans to proceed with the buildup of conventional ground forces thus progressively diminished. The development of the German army proceeded slowly mainly on paper, impeded by an increasing undertow of reluctance. By the end of 1956 the initial concept of NATO, which had reached its peak of influence at the Lisbon meetings in February 1952 (with force goals of approximately 100 divisions for 1954), was virtually dead.

The second factor influencing this evolution was the change in Soviet strategy which began to take shape in the summer of 1951, and rapidly gathered momentum after Stalin's death in March 1953. This strategy recognized that, whatever Communist gains from the Korean war may have been, the American and United Nations reaction to overt Communist aggression was, on balance, exceedingly costly to the Soviets; and that there were greater possibilities for the extension of communism by political, psychological, and economic means which would associate communism with peace, nationalism, and economic progress. In Asia, the Middle East, and Africa, to which this policy was mainly directed, the new Soviet tactic met a considerable response, backed as it was by the blackmailing threat of rising Soviet military strength relative to the United States. In Europe as well it had some effect in convincing Europeans that further military effort within the context of NATO was not merely of doubtful value but of diminished urgency. In the case of Germany, Soviet diplomacy sharply dramatized the idea that German unity could be achieved only by a definitive break with NATO and the United States. In November 1956 the use of limited force in the Middle East and in Hungary again raised in Europe the possibility of limited war within the framework of atomic stalemate; and it stimulated the Germans especially to look to the development of some ground forces. But, as the crisis of November 1956 rolled on, no clear and generally accepted military concept of NATO's role in a world of H-bombs had yet emerged.

A final set of eroding forces developed in the underdeveloped areas of Asia, the Middle East, and Africa. The pattern of American and free world alliances designed to maintain deterrent force in being against Communist capabilities for limited war progressively clashed in three separate dimensions with the interests of our partners as they came to see those interests. In the SEATO area (notably on the Asian mainland) Thailand, Laos, and Cambodia began to doubt that a military buildup of their own forces without an American commitment to maintain troops on the spot constituted a persuasive deterrent to Communist ground-force strength mounted across their borders in China. With the possible exception of South Korea, it was evidently impossible to build sufficient local strength to deal with potential Chinese Communist force; and so Laos and Cambodia began to look to bilateral accommodation with Peking and Moscow, an accommodation which was made superficially attractive by the current phase of Communist world policy.

Second, as the apparent danger of direct Communist military aggression receded, the pursuit of other political aspirations of the new nations and colonial areas rose in priority. The Pakistani increasingly thought of Kashmir rather than of the threat from the north; the Egyptians began to project their weight into north and central Africa and toward the formation of a Middle East bloc; the issue of colonialism in French North Africa came to a head; the Bagdad Pact became essentially a move in free world power diplomacy rather than a ground-force deterrent against Communist military strength. This assertion of believed national interests within the underdeveloped regions further disrupted the pattern of Asian and Middle East military alliances and had consequences for the Western European powers which further weakened the coherence and effectiveness of NATO.

Finally, the sense of urgency about economic development increased in the underdeveloped areas and, with it, the attractiveness of economic rather than military assistance from the United States. Even in the SEATO area the pressures for increased economic aid expanded; and elsewhere in the underdeveloped areas the continued American emphasis on the maintenance of the ground-force deterrence against limited war appeared out of key with local political pressures and interests. Our allies, friends, and potential friends in the underdeveloped areas of the free world became progressively more frustrated by the cast of American policy and the aid programs that backed it.

LONG-RUN DEVELOPMENT ASSISTANCE

At the Bretton Woods Conference of July 1944 the representatives of what were to be later known as the underdeveloped areas urged strongly that the International Bank be used not merely for medium term reconstuction but also for long-run economic development. This pressure arose mainly from representatives of the countries of Latin America, but they spoke as well for the existing and incipient nations of Asia, the Middle East, and Africa. Although the immediate postwar years were dominated by events in Europe, in the Councils of the United Nations the underdeveloped areas steadily pressed their case for loans and technical assistance from the richer, more industrialized nations. There was deep resentment at the enormous sums being allocated by the United States to sustain Europe at relatively high standards of welfare while their peoples languished in extreme poverty.

Responding to this pressure, the United Nations Assembly meeting in the winter of 1948 set in motion the United Nations technical assistance program, and President Truman presented his fourth point in his inaugural address of January 20, 1949:

> Fourth. We must embark on a bold new program for making the benefits of our scientific advances and industrial progress available for the improvement and growth of underdeveloped areas. . . .

The character of the American national stake in the economic growth of the underdeveloped areas was somewhat vaguely articulated by President Truman. He leaned mainly on a combination of humanitarianism and American economic self-interest, but, also, in general terms, linked successful economic development to the conditions for peace and the spread of the democratic process. There was a similar vagueness about the concrete economic objectives of the program and the scale of the American effort required to produce a meaningful result in terms of American interests. In the upshot, the fourth-point program was launched on a modest scale and almost wholly in terms of technical assistance.

The importance of the underdeveloped areas of the world to the American interest, and the need to meet their powerful aspirations for the modernization of their societies, were increasingly appreciated in 1949-50; European recovery had gathered momentum, and the military position there appeared to be stabilized, but communism had moved to a victory in China which shadowed the free world's prospects throughout Asia. Gordon Gray's report to the President on Foreign Economic Policies, in November 1950, and Nelson Rockefeller's Partners in Progress report of March 1951 reflected a growing awareness of the strategic importance to the United States of long-run development in the underdeveloped areas.

Rightly or wrongly, it was judged that economic assistance could only be justified persuasively to the Congress and the American people on literal grounds of the American military interest. Very substantial economic assistance in the form of military support went to areas linked to the United States by military treaty; but only a small proportion of the population of the underdeveloped areas of the world shared substantially in American aid. Moreover, in the treaty areas (notably, Korea, Vietnam, Taiwan, and Pakistan) the conditions under which this aid was granted—linked as it was to the maintenance of military forces much larger than could be supported by the economies of these countries—diverted energy, administrative talent, and resources away from the tasks of long-term economic development.

While the broad considerations of national interest incorporated in the initial rationale for the fourth-point program were widely accepted in the Government and in official pronouncements, and although the program was steadily maintained at a modest level, its role in American strategy on the world scene was never clearly defined in the public's mind. The Nation persisted in programs designed to deter limited war, while Communist policy took on new dimensions.

There was no lack of awareness in the Congress concerning the positive character of the American interest in associating our policies with the desire of peoples in the underdeveloped areas for that degree of economic development needed to underpin and to give substance to their high aspirations for independence, democracy, and increased human dignity. For example, Public Law 726, passed by the 84th Congress, contains this passage:

> Section 14. It is the sense of Congress that, in the preparation of the mutual security program, the President should take fully into account the desirability of affirmatively promoting the economic de-

velopment of underdeveloped countries, both as a means of effectively counteracting the increased political and economic emphasis of Soviet foreign policy and as a means of promoting fundamental American foreign-policy objectives of political and economic self-determination and independence.

What was in question at the end of 1956 was whether the scale and character of the existing aid program fulfilled the large objective it was designed to support.

CONCLUSION

What can we conclude from this sequence about the underlying objectives of American aid since the end of the Second World War? In general terms, the Congress has consistently recognized that in the world that has emerged after the Second World War the United States must actively use its economic resources to help maintain a world environment—military and political—which will permit our free society to continue to develop along lines congenial with our history and our hopes for the future. As the Second World War drew to a close, we were generous with our wartime friends and with the peoples in the enemy countries because we sensed that, unless they got back on their feet economically, they would, at best, be incapable of playing a part in a peaceful, orderly world; and, at worst, in desperation, they might reach out for Communist or other nondemocratic solutions to their acute problems.

When Stalin's intentions in Europe became clear in 1947, the Soviet threat to the world environment of the United States became urgent; and we threw our resources into the economic and then the military rehabilitation of Europe. In the Marshall plan and NATO (as in the First and Second World Wars) we recognized that the loss of Europe to a hostile power was a direct security threat to the United States. More than that, we recognized that Europe could be lost not merely by the march of Soviet troops from eastern Europe to the Channel but by the loss of confidence among Europeans that adherence to the democratic process was compatible with their continued economic progress.

As regards the underdeveloped areas of Asia, the Middle East, and Africa, we have recognized in principle from Bretton Woods forward that, in some sense, their economic progress, their independence, and their evolution toward democracy mattered to us;

and in 1949-50 there was evidence that this perspective was being crystallized out in American thought and might lead on to the development of a new American policy toward the underdeveloped areas. The Korean war intervened, however, and in its aftermath the effort to hold the balance of power favorable to the free world in Asia, the Middle East, and Africa has mainly taken a military or quasi-military form.

Since the end of the Korean war the effectiveness of this military method—taken by itself—has been progressively put in question; by the changing character of our military problem vis-à-vis the Soviet Union and Communist China; by the character of the strategy pursued by Moscow and Peking; and by the changing psychological attitudes and rising political ambitions of the nations of the underdeveloped areas. Congress has evidently been aware of these changes, and that awareness can be seen, to a degree, in the changing regional direction and character of our aid programs. But the nature of the American problem of holding power for the free world in Asia, the Middle East, and Africa has altered more radically than our policies and the aid programs designed to give them substance.

In short, we still lack in the underdeveloped areas an equivalent to the balanced economic-military approach represented (down to 1952) in Europe by the Marshall plan and NATO.

In a more basic sense we have not yet clarified our national interest in the underdeveloped areas, the character of the military and economic jobs that now need to be done there, and the scale and manner in which our national resources should be mobilized to help do those jobs.

III

Foreign Aid: An Emotion-Packed Argument

About the Readings

The selection by Eugene Castle demonstrates the highly charged nature of the debate on foreign aid. Although he happens to be one who opposes aid with high emotional fervor, there are many who support it with a similar degree of spirit. The extensive spending of tax money for "foreign" purposes seems to raise the hackles of many proponents and opponents alike.

The next selection is a detailed reply to Mr. Castle's charges by the International Cooperation Administration (the United States agency which administers much of the foreign aid). While the emotion is fairly well concealed in the reply, it is fairly easy to imagine the spirit with which the governmental officials attacked the job of attempting to refute Mr. Castle's charges. Whether they succeed is a matter for analysis and opinion.

Both selections may be taken as warnings to be on guard against the sweeping statement and the apparent common sense of any of the positions. There may be more than two sides to every story.

FOREIGN SPREE FOR OUR SUPERSPENDERS*

EUGENE W. CASTLE

EUGENE W. CASTLE *was a frequent contributor to various magazines and author of* Billions, Blunders and Baloney *(New York: Devin-Adair, 1955), a highly critical account of our foreign-aid programs. He died February 9, 1960, in New York.*

Once again, from Washington, come the familiar pleas for more money to spend, tied to whatever current excuse will serve to frighten the American people into substituting spending for orderly progress and common sense. Ignored is the fact that a strong economy is still the most powerful weapon for our survival. Yet inflation, always the end product of reckless spending, could fulfill the prediction of Lenin in 1920 that America would be conquered —because we eventually would spend ourselves into bankruptcy. . . .

We do not have the resources permanently to support all men everywhere. The real meaning of the NATO meeting in Paris last December was that our allies told us that they had little faith in our ideas and were even reluctant to agree to accept more of our global bribery. Instead, they urged us to go to Moscow and make a "talk" deal with the Kremlin. Yet, we are again being urged to perpetuate these same ill-conceived and badly executed schemes and policies that weaken our economy and dissipate our resources under the false assumption that we can buy allies with bales of money—and convert them with torrents of worthless propaganda.

Since the Soviets respect only strength, none will disagree that there must be concentration on our missile program and other means of maintaining military power. This does not mean, however, that those who spend our money should be allowed to use any excuse to waste our Nation's resources on other projects. Both prudence and self-interest dictate that, if we are to survive against the slave states, we must find ways and means to get the maximum value for every dollar expanded.

One thing is certain. The solution to our problems is not to

* Reprinted from *The American Mercury,* May 1958. Copyright, 1958, *The American Mercury.*

be found in circling the globe with more foreign-aid dollars. Foreign aid is now the second-largest operating item in our Federal budget. By July 1, 1958, our foreign-aid ventures will approximate the astronomical total of $70 billion.

So anxious are they to keep the giving in high gear that our highest officials continually fly around the world seeking new ways and means of maintaining and enlarging this global giving.

Basically our foreign-aid program was conceived as the unselfish action of a successful nation to rescue the devasted countries of Europe from the ravages of war. That objective, originally estimated to cost not more than $17 billion and to be completed within 4 years, was accomplished. Those who conceived it did not intend that it should continue for 13 years and $70 billion.

Few will dispute that a limited amount of foreign aid honestly and carefully dispensed to such friends as Turkey, Greece, Formosa, and Korea is justifiable; but the idea of continuing to try to buy the friendship of nations is completely unsound.

Presently, our foreign-aid bill billions are paid mostly to the governments or public authorities of the receiving countries. Very large sums of our aid moneys allocated freely to underdeveloped countries all too often find their way into the pockets of the ruling politicians and their supporters. Some countries use our aid dollars to pay for luxury imports. Others spend our money for a multitude of unwanted public-works projects.

Let us recall a few of these projects: Our foreign aiders financed an extensive survey to ascertain the sexual habits of Nehru's Indians. . . .

In Lebanon, our foreign aid dollars are used to plant wild grass shoots along public highways. . . .

We have provided dress suits for Grecian undertakers, public baths for Egyptian camel drivers and free airplane rides for thousands of Arabs to visit their religious shrine in Mecca.

In the name of foreign aid we are spending $5 million annually to send warblers of arias to Western Europe, weight lifters to the Near East, and high-priced jazz bands to the Far East. . . .

For the past several years, Secretary of State John Foster Dulles repeatedly has assured us that the Soviet economy was becoming worse by the hour and that it was on the verge of a crackup. Now, Mr. Dulles does a sudden and complete about face. He solemnly warns congressional committees and issues lengthy press releases to the American people to inform us that the now affluent Soviet bloc is tripping over itself in outgiving us in economic handouts and that if we do not immediately enter a marathon to match this alleged and recently discovered Red generosity we are most certainly destined toward ruin.

As part of Washington's stepped up campaign to terrify the American public into supporting bigger foreign giveaways than ever, the State Department recently announced that during 1956 and 1957 the Soviet bloc agreed to supply $1.9 billion of military and economic assistance to 10 underdeveloped countries while during the same period the United States allocated only $900 million to these countries.

This sudden announcement, made just before Congress reconvened, is wholly misleading.

The facts are that out of the total of $1.9 billion which the State Department gave as an estimate, the Soviet bloc promised $1,335 million and earmarked—but did not deliver—this sum for four countries, Egypt, Yugoslavia, Syria, and Indonesia. All of these countries can be classed as frigidly unfriendly to us and what we stand for. Only 10 to 15 percent of the promised Soviet money—that is between $130 and $170 million—has been actually spent in these countries. During the same years of 1956 and 1957, the United States provided nonmilitary aid to the Middle East and Asia amounting to more than $2 billion, or more than 10 times the Soviet payoff. In addition, very large quantities of military aid, logistic supplies and free food were ladled out by our global givers during this 2-year period.

If, as we are now told, the Soviets can accomplish so much by giving so little away, then why have we accomplished so little while giving so much? Actually, we are far outspending the Soviet bloc on both economic and military aid. Our real concern lies in getting much better value for what we are now giving away rather than making additional and unwarranted billions available to our self-perpetuated planners.

At one time only nations that appeared to be friendly were eligible for our foreign aid. Neutralists were to get nothing. But our Washington bureaucrats could not muster up enough friendly nations so the rules were mysteriously changed to enable neutralists —and even Communists—to receive the billions wrung from the American taxpayers. . . .

It has just been revealed that the International Cooperation Administration finds itself in the embarrassing position of not yet having spent the $300 million included in this year's budget—now the ICA is doing handsprings to get rid of these hundreds of millions before double this amount is made available for the new fiscal year. Secretary Dulles went to Baghdad to get rid of some of this money quickly and ICA Director Smith has been flying around the Near East trying to do the same before the June 30 fiscal deadline.

Under Secretary of State Douglas Dillon, now the coordinator of foreign aid, has, for many months, been actively seeking to obtain a substantial increase in the blank check allocation. Dillon, with the backing of both the President and the Secretary of State, has called for the immediate availability of $625 million which Congress specified in the Mutual Security Act of 1957 could not be spent before the fiscal year beginning July 1958. The spending of these hundreds of millions far ahead of schedule would, of course, facilitate the fulfillment of the promise made to Nehru, and, at the same time, would avoid a bitter and prolonged debate in Congress. But it would also nullify the intent of Congress. . . .

The President and those who advice and speak for him, appear unaware of the conclusions reached by industrial adviser to the International Cooperation Administration in India who said:

"Our extreme vulnerability here (India) seems to me to be in the fact that we are trying to do is unknown to 80 or 85 percent of the population and only known to at the most 15 percent of the population, the political leaders and educated people who manipulate or suppress this knowledge to suit their political motives of the moment. . . . Two facts may be accepted without question: India is determined to socialize or nationalize all industry as soon as possible, and there exist more offers of aid from sources other than the United States than India can possibly assimilate or accept. Now, why do we use the American taxpayers' money to accelerate nationalization of industry in India? The time has passed when they can be converted to private enterprise and all we are buying is a minority interest or liability in a national policy that is ultimately headed for either economic chaos or communism."

In the case of Yugoslavia and Poland, our aid dollars are not even buying a minority interest in a liability. They are actually reducing the liabilities of those who unqualifiedly support the men in the Kremlin and whose avowed purpose was and is to destroy us. Red Dictator Tito and Moscow's Polish puppet, Gomulka, both openly boast that they are and will continue to be bedfellows of the men in the Kremlin. Yet, despite the pronouncements and actions of these two avowed Communists, new excuses are being found to pressure both the Congress and the American people into sending more hundreds of millions after the vast sums already wasted.

Nehru, Tito, and Gomulka are but three examples of how the American taxpayers could and should be saved hundreds of millions of wasted dollars, and these savings should be made now.

Four years ago there were 9,793 persons on the Government's foreign aid payrolls. Today there are 18,819 employed in our ICA, State, and Defense Departments, to give our resources away. Yet Congress reduced the billions for foreign aid spending from $6 billion in 1953 to $3.5 billions for the current fiscal year. With fewer billions to spend, why do we need twice the number of people to spend them?

If the ICA were to cut down on its field programs, reduce the number of bodies serving it in Washington and throughout the world, two things would happen: The rank and scale of pay of the great mass of officials would be dropped one or more grades, and the still greater mob of jobholders would be substantially reduced. Obviously this will never be done voluntarily by thousands of people who have become careerists and paymasters in the disposal of $5 billion annually and who, as a group, never had it so good. Our Chief Executive and those who plead for him insist upon perpetuating and not reducing this wasteful and topheavy bureaucracy.

Perhaps too many of us are under the erroneous impression that the Government's perpetual spending for foreign aid is very far away in terms of our own personal economy. But in reality, this is not so. Foreign aid is much closer to our everyday life than most of us realize. Year after year, since the end of the war, our foreign aid expenditures represented our deficit financing. Now there are the added dangers of the national debt already revised and the return to a deficit economy. To continue the annual spending of more than $5 billion (which includes our food giveaway of one billion annually) will make impossible for many years to come a balanced budget with sufficient surplus to provide tax reduction for millions of middle-bracket Americans. . . .

Those who clamor for more foreign aid never mention the fact that our giveaway program has already cost us twice as much as all Social Security benefits, plus aid to the needy, aged, blind, and disabled. And it has cost three times as much as all farm programs since the war, and seven times as much as all atomic energy projects.

The $70 billion total for foreign aid spending, which we are now approaching, is the equivalent of one-fourth of our present national debt. The cost of servicing this portion of the debt now approximates $2 billion annually, or one-fourth of the total interest charge. This is a continuing expense. . . .

Year after year, as appropriation time approaches, the administration, its spokesmen, and manipulated pressure groups discover new pretexts to pressure the Congress and propagandize the American people. Last year it was Egypt and Syria. The year before it was the Russian loans (not gifts) to Afghanistan, Burma, and India. Sputnik was promoted as the excuse for hiking the foreign-aid bill by more than a billion dollars and to increase the lending authority of the Export-Import Bank for an additional $2 billion.

Despite bureaucratic pressures, we must not permit foreign aid, presently the cornerstone of our foreign policy, to become the tombstone of our Nation. Instead, foreign aid should now be tapered off so that eventually millions will be used to observed advantage where billions are presently being wasted. Americans would then have a foreign-aid bill from Congress which our Republic could support, one that would no longer be a device for politicians to use for promoting themselves as WPA directors of the world.

Last year when the President confronted the Nation with a bloated $71 billion budget, the people showered their protests upon Washington to an extent never experienced before. The avalanche of mail hitting Capitol Hill, demanding a deep cut in foreign-aid appropriations, caused panic in the White House as well as in the offices of Senators who were attempting to defend the continuance of unlimited giveaway funds and the maintenance of rivers of waste and extravagance.

Our businesswise citizens must tell their Congressmen again and again that economy and integrity in Government are still the greatest weapons we possess. Responsive to the will of the people, Congress if commanded will reduce foreign aid, which visibly is yielding diminishing results.

THE INTERNATIONAL
COOPERATION
ADMINISTRATION REPLIES*

BY THE ICA

The International Cooperation Administration is the United States governmental agency which is assigned the responsibility of administering American aid programs.

Charge No. 2 continued: . . . (b) The mutual security program is based on the false assumption that we can buy allies with bales of money.

Answer: (b) The mutual security program does not seek to buy friends and allies for dollars, and any program with such a purpose is doomed to fail. As has been repeated time and again by the leaders of both political parties, the program is designed to enhance our national security. It is achieving this end: it has checked the advance of Communist imperialism most dramatically in Greece, Iran, and Vietnam; by defraying about 20 percent of the cost, it has provided armed forces of 5 million men joined with ours through collective security agreements; it has enabled us to secure and maintain 250 bases vital to our air and naval forces; and in the face of Communist pressure and blandishments, through economic and technical assistance, it has enabled the many new but underdeveloped nations to maintain their independence and to begin the economic development their people so desire and deserve.

The countries to which we extend military and economic aid are not our satellites to which we dictate domestic and foreign policies, nor is it our desire to make them such. They are rather free and independent nations, and thus many honestly differ with us on many issues. But they all agree with us on the fundamental issue: the need for a truly peaceful world in which nations are free to pursue their destinies in their own way. By helping establish security from aggression and in the underdeveloped nations, providing hope

* Reprinted from *U.S. Congressional Record,* 85th Congress, 2nd Session, 1958, 10143-10154.

for economic betterment, this program encourages and enables countries to continue working toward their goals through free and democratic institutions. . . .

Charge No. 4: Mr. Eugene Castle states: "Presently, our foreign-aid billions are paid mostly to the governments or public authorities of the receiving countries. Very large sums of our aid moneys allocated freely to underdeveloped countries all too often find their way into the pockets of the ruling politicians and their supporters."

Answer: Mutual security funds almost never take the form of dollars "paid" to governments and public authorities of receiving countries. Rather, it is the supply of goods and technicians. In the case of goods, these are provided normally through commercial channels and, while there may be opportunities for indirect gain on the part of government officials, the aid dollars themselves cannot result directly in personal gain. The providing of technicians, of course, gives no opportunities of this kind. In the 10 years of mutual security and predecessor programs in the economic field, totaling over $20 billion, there is a remarkable record of honesty in the handling of these programs. What minor instances of alleged charges of misuse have occurred are either unsubstantiated or in a few instances involve the actions of government officials which are beyond the control of this government. And again it is noted in these cases it is not the aid dollars themselves which are available for misuse. . . .

Question No. 5: Are any of our foreign aid dollars used to pay for luxury imports by the recipient countries?

Answer: Under ICA policies United States assistance may not be used for importing luxury items. ICA has taken careful steps to enforce these policies and thereby to make sure that this does not happen. These steps include: (1) the building up over the years of an internal administrative list of specific items classed as luxuries which in the absence of a demonstration of their essentiality are not eligible for ICA financing, (2) a careful system of end use checks or checks on the actual use to which United States-financed imports are put, (3) an arrival accounting system operated either by the United States or by the host government which in turn makes reports to us, and (4) a system of penalties for any infraction of the policy against luxuries under which the United States money so used is recaptured.

Charges of this sort are made from time to time because observers learn of certain imports but do not learn of the use to which they are put. For example, one might make this charge about air conditioners or cameras. But it is apparent than an air conditioner is not a luxury where laboratory work requires rigid temperature control. Similarly, what may appear under the label "camera" is not a luxury item if it is a specialized type of industrial photographic equipment. These are two actual examples of charges which have been made. This kind of charge frequently occurs also when the observer learns of the existence within a country of luxury items and makes this charge without learning that, in fact, no mutual security funds were used to finance its import.

Obviously, no administrative system can prevent mistakes. This is particularly true where, as required by law (as well as sound principle), we make maximum use of private trade channels. But if an unauthorized use is made of ICA funds, the aid country is obliged to make a refund of such funds to ICA. As of January 31, 1958, over $8 million had been received by ICA from aid countries as refunds of amounts improperly spent for luxury or unessential goods. . . .

Question No. 12: (a) Are we financing the planting of wild grass roots along public highways in Lebanon? (b) If so, why? (c) What is the value of this project?

Answer: (a) We have contributed the services of a technician and the use of two tractors to a project involving the planting of wild grass shoots along a Lebanese highway.

(b) The purpose of this project was to prevent movement of sand. The highway in question runs from Beirut to the Khalde airport. Winds from the sea were blowing sand over the highway from adjacent dunes. This sand movement constituted a serious traffic hazard, not only to highway traffic but to incoming aircraft as well. It is estimated that annual labor costs of removing sand from the road were $16,000. It was considered that this was a worthwhile project to further by contributing technical guidance and equipment.

(c) The project as a whole cost approximately $4,000. ICA's contribution consisted of the part-time services of 1 technician and use of 2 tractors, both in the area in connection with other ICA-financed projects. The Government of Lebanon provided the other equipment, fuel, lubricants, grass shoots, and labor.

Although this was not treated as a separate ICA project, the work done was highly successful and nearby countries have drawn upon Lebanese experience to tackle similar dune-control problems. This is an excellent example of the sort of incidental assistance which is possible within an aid-receiving country at little or no additional cost to the United States. . . .

Question No. 19: Have we financed public baths for Egyptian camel drivers?

Answer: ICA has provided funds to assist a cooperative rural health demonstration center at Shubra Mont, in Egypt. The project included public baths as part of the health center. Although the project commodity procurement schedule, which describes the commodities being brought with the United States dollar contributions to the project, does not include public baths, some of the commodities procured could have been used in connection with building the baths.

There is also included as part of the Egyptian-American rural improvement service projects a project for village improvement in the Abis area. This project which was financed from a joint United States-Egyptian joint fund provided for the construction of a building combining baths and a laundry.

Neither of these projects was specifically designed to provide facilities for camel drivers. However, it is obviously possible that the facilities could have been used by camel drivers. This is particularly true of the Shubra Mont project, which is located just off a well-traveled road to Cairo.

The inclusion of public bathing facilities in these two projects results from the fact that Egyptian villages customarily have public bathing facilities, and from the further fact that such facilities are frequently no more than drainage ditches, the use of which has sometimes led to the development of bilharzia. A project designed to encourage and improve health and sanitation standards would therefore necessarily include public bathing facilities.

It should be pointed out, furthermore, that technical cooperation projects have for some time included public bathing facilities in health projects. . . .

Question No. 21: Are foreign aid funds being used to send operatic singers to Western Europe, weight lifters to the Middle East, and jazz bands to Latin America and the Far East?

Answer: No.

Some tours abroad by creative and performing artists and ath-
letes from the United States are being assisted by the Department of
State under the express authority of Public Law 860, 84th Congress.
They are not a part of the mutual-security program and are not administered by ICA. . . .

Charge No. 33: (a) Statement: "Our extreme vulnerability here
[India] seems to me to be in the fact that what we are trying to do
is unknown to 80 or 85 percent of the population and only known
to at the most 15 percent of the population, the political leaders
and educated people who manipulate or suppress this knowledge to
suit their political motives of the moment. . . . Two facts may be
accepted without question: India is determined to socialize or
nationalize all industry as soon as possible, and there exist more
offers of aid from sources other than the United States than India
can possibly assimilate or accept."

Answer: The assertion that the political leaders and educated
people of India manipulate or suppress knowledge of the United
States aid program is not supported by any evidence.

India, as a democracy, has a free press, which has always carried
news stories about United States aid to India. Official Indian Government publications give credit to United States assistance where
appropriate. For example, the reports of the Estimates Committee
of the Parliament recognize explicitly the role the United States
had in helping to initiate the community development program in
India. The Explanatory Memorandum on the Budget of the Central
Government of India for 1958-59 contains throughout the document
notations and references to United States assistance. Prime Minister
Nehru, at the general conference of 200 mission personnel November 20, 1957, put it this way:

> "We welcome your cooperation here, your assistance, your part-
> nership in this tremendous adventure in India. We are grateful, not
> only today, but for the last many years, for the assistance in various
> ways which we have received from the United States."

We would not presume to guess how many people in this nation
of almost 400 million people know about the United States aid
program. Some 80 percent of the population live in rural and agricultural areas; perhaps 20 percent of the people are literate. We
feel certain that some of the programs in which ICA has participated, such as community development and malaria control and

eradication, are known to most of the Indian population literate or not. . . .

Question No. 34: "In the case of Yugoslavia and Poland, our aid dollars are not even buying a minority interest in a liability. They are actually reducing the liabilities of those who unqualifiedly support the men in the Kremlin and whose avowed purpose was and is to destroy us. Red Dictator Tito and Moscow's Polish puppet, Gomulka, both openly boast that they are and will continue to be bedfellows of the men in the Kremlin. Yet, despite the pronouncements and actions of these two avowed Communists, new excuses are being found to pressure both the Congress and the American people into sending more hundreds of millions after the vast sums already wasted.

"Nehru, Tito, and Gomulka are but three examples of how the American taxpayers could and should be saved hundreds of millions of wasted dollars, and these savings should be made now."

Answer: 1. Yugoslavia:

The economic assistance which we have provided to Yugoslavia under this program in recent years and that which we now propose serves one overriding purpose. It helps Yugoslavia to maintain its independent status. As the first Communist country to assert such independence of the U.S.S.R., Yugoslavia has exercised and continues to exercise an influence in Eastern Europe out of all proportion to its size.

The determination of Yugoslav leaders, moreover, to maintain their independence and to resist Soviet efforts to reassert domination over them has apparently not been shaken. This was demonstrated in November 1957, when the Yugoslavs refused to sign the Moscow declaration of principles issued on the occasion of the 40th anniversary of the Bolshevik revolution. It was demonstrated even more forcefully at the recent Yugoslav Party Congress in Ljubljana, where Tito and his colleagues defied Soviet attacks and a boycott of the meetings to approve a party program which had been sharply criticized as erroneous and inaccurate by Soviet leaders. The basic issue between Yugoslavia and the Soviet Union is of course Yugoslavia's refusal to accept Soviet domination. From this there have evolved, however, some rather liberal reforms (e.g. the breakup of collective farms and the introduction of workers' councils) which have had an influence on the thinking in other Communist countries.

In a word, the essential consideration which motivates our policy with respect to Yugoslavia and the mutual security program is not whether we agree with that country's political and economic philosophy but whether we want it to be able to stay independent.

Yugoslavia, currently engaged in a renewed struggle with the Kremlin, is scheduled to receive some further economic aid in the form of special assistance and a small technical cooperation program in fiscal year 1959. No great military assistance is proposed. In December, at Yugoslav initiative, further deliveries of military aid were halted, and discussions were undertaken for the termination of the entire grant military assistance program. We do not exclude the possibility of some further sales of military equipment to Yugoslavia, however. . . .

Charge No. 36: (a) "Perhaps too many of us are under the erroneous impression that the Government's perpetual spending for foreign aid is very far away in terms of our own personal economy. But in reality, this is not so. Foreign aid is much closer to our everyday life than most of us realize. Year after year, since the end of the war, our foreign-aid expenditures represented our deficit financing. Now there are the added dangers of the national debt already revised and the return to a deficit economy. To continue the annual spending of more than $5 billion (which includes our food giveaway of 1 billion annually) will make impossible for many years to come a balanced budget with sufficient surplus to provide tax reduction for millions of middle-bracket Americans, who are sadly in need of such assistance."

(b) "Those who clamor for more foreign aid never mention the fact that our giveaway program has already cost us twice as much as all social security benefits, plus aid to the needy, aged, blind, and disabled. And it has cost three times as much as all farm programs since the war and seven times as much as all atomic-energy projects."

(c) "The $70 billion total for foreign aid spending, which we are now approaching, is the equivalent of one-fourth of our present national debt. The cost of servicing this portion of the debt now approximates $2 billion annually, or one-fourth of the total interest charge. This is a continuing expense."

Answer: (a) The public debt of the United States rose from $252.3 billion on June 30, 1948, to $270.5 billion on June 30, 1957, a net increase of $18.2 billion. It is not possible to attribute any one part of the increase in the public debt to a particular type of expenditure of the Federal Government. It should be observed, however, that during the 3-year period of heavy expenditures in connection with the Korean war, December 1950 to December 1953, the national debt rose from $256.7 billion to $275.2 billion.

(b) The expenditures of the Federal Government for the several programs cited for the period July 1, 1948, through June 30, 1957, are as follows:

	Billion
1. Social security plus aid to the aged, blind and disabled	$59.2
2. Farm programs	26.4
3. Atomic energy	13.1

The cost of the mutual-security program from April 1948 through June 30, 1957, is as follows:

	Billion
1. Military Assistance (grants)	$20.1
2. Economic Assistance (grants and loans)	22.5
TOTAL	42.6

(c) It is possible to relate mutual security expenditures to total Federal expenditures during the period and then prorate part of the increase to the mutual-security program. During the period from July 1, 1948, through June 30, 1957, total budget expenditures of the Federal Government were $531.1 billion. For the same period, the cost of the mutual-security program (military and economic) was $42.6 billion. On a pro rata basis, the mutual-security program accounts for 8 percent of total Federal Government expenditures. On this basis about $1.5 billion of the total debt increase of $18.2 billion is accounted for by the mutual-security program. . . .

IV

The Morality of Foreign Aid: The Humanitarian Ideal and a Moral Criterion

About the Readings

This section is focused primarily on the opposing poles of the question of whether the moral obligations of the United States should extend outward into the international arena, with an attempt to help raise living standards internationally, or should remain chiefly within our borders, with an increased attempt to take care of its own people first. Although, in reality, this may be a false dichotomy, with only an extremely small number of people at either of the extremes, the problem of what the emphasis should be is very real indeed. Thus, this section deserves careful analysis.

The first selection, by Paul Homan, was written in response to a request to indicate the most important economic problem facing the United States in the next twenty years. What seems to be his rationale for emphasizing the moral aspect in our relations with other countries?

The next selection, a statement by Waldo Chamberlin on behalf of the National Council of Churches of Christ in the U.S.A., seems to be representative of the opinion of various church organizations in the country on the matter of foreign aid. Note the similarity between his general position and that of Professor Homan. Can any important differences be detected?

The third article, by Edward F. Snyder, contains a variation on the morality theme. His interpretation of the moral thing to do with foreign aid indicates an important difference with Mr. Chamberlin over the strategy and perhaps the objectives of foreign aid. Both men start on the moral premise that humanity is indivisible. Where do they part company? Why?

Up to this point the section has been concerned mainly with an examination of the moral principles for supporting American foreign-aid activities. The next article, by Spruille Braden, deals with the morality of opposition to the foreign-aid programs. Although this viewpoint may not be taken by the majority of scholars, it certainly is held by a significant number of people in the United States. (For a differing and opposing view, the reader is referred to Irving Kristol, "The Ideology of Economic Aid," Yale Review, Summer 1957).

ECONOMIC RELATIONS WITH
OTHER COUNTRIES*

PAUL T. HOMAN

PAUL T. HOMAN, *Professor of Economics at the University of California, Los Angeles, and former editor of the* American Economic Review, *is a frequent contributor to various magazines and periodicals and author of several books in economics.*

The most important problems facing the United States lie in the sphere of this country's relations with other countries. These problems are by no means all primarily economic in character—the attainment and maintenance of peace, though not at any price, outrank all others—but an economic element interpenetrates them all, and in some the economic element predominates. Of these latter, to my mind the most crucial and far-reaching is the extent of the willingness of the United States to assist the poorer and less stable countries to improve their situations with mutually beneficial purposes. I shall approach the defense of this thesis by a somewhat roundabout route.

A characteristic of what we call economic problems is that they are never "strictly economic." It is often convenient to apply strict economic criteria in order to isolate aspects of a problem for the purposes of analysis. But as soon as one enters the cluster of problems involving conflicts of interest—in particular, the distribution of income—questions of social ends and social morality invariably intrude. The mounting productivity of the American economy is pushing scarcity into the background, except for scarcity of raw materials which calls for greater international interdependence. Consequently, many of our problems have to be reformulated in terms of what to do with our plenty. In this environment, domestic questions of equity in distribution and of social relations in production do not disappear, but they cease to have the urgency they once had.

This comfortable state of affairs is dependent, of course, on the ability to maintain the economy on a fairly even keel and to support

* Reprinted from *Problems of U.S. Economic Development,* Vol. I (New York: Committee for Economic Development, 1958), pp. 21-32.

a satisfactory rate of growth and level of employment. The ability to do this cannot be taken for granted, and one could easily argue that our greatest economic problem is to ensure the continuance of this condition. I shall, however, assume our capacity to whip this problem by a combination of economic wisdom and political sagacity. In a stable and increasingly productive economy, our thinking will have to be concerned more and more with how to make a state of rising economic plenty contribute to human well-being. We shall have to envisage new ends and the means appropriate thereto.

Applying this approach to the domestic scene, the problems are, in the broadest sense, cultural. That is to say, once the pressure of the more obvious economic needs has been removed, it has to be determined how a mounting capacity to produce can be made to serve the higher qualities of man—to increase his "dignity and worth." Many of these problems are in a high degree personal and any solution lies within the realm of voluntary choice. Others, however, are in high degree collective, relating to ways and means of improving the physical, social and cultural environment within which our personal lives are lived and our tastes and values formed. The importance of these problems is not downgraded by emphasis upon international relationships. In the end, the same principles are applicable in both areas.

The upward striving of the human race depends upon attitudes; and I do not think a satisfactory state of civilization can be achieved in the United States so long as it entertains a tribal attitude toward the rest of the human race. There was perhaps a time when, in historic perspective, it was defensible to pursue "the promise of American life" in isolation. If so, the time is past and is generally recognized to be past. Since we must perforce pursue our destiny as a member of the world community—and as in many respects its leading member—we have necessarily to redefine the terms of our participation.

At present the participation is reluctant and the tendency is to make it as narrow as immediate circumstances permit—to define it almost exclusively in terms of "national security." The "realists" in the sphere of international relations assure us that this is all that can be expected from public opinion as reflected in the Congress. Even if this is so, much more could be done than is now being done on that principle toward supporting the aspirations of other countries for economic improvement. But the long-run question facing the United States is made clearer by asking what responsibilities we ought to assume if the cold war was over and there were no security reason for extending aid. The tribal answer is, "no responsibility." This is an unsatisfactory answer even on the narrow economic grounds of the principle of comparative advantage; and even less so on broader social grounds. Tribal attitudes are not all to be denigrated. They provide a focus for group loyalties, and if the values which these attitudes support have merit, they can be steps on the ladder of civilization. But they are more commonly the carriers of the barbaric traits and the vehicles of those who seek and abuse irresponsible power. In the United States, as elsewhere, they are often the raw materials of demagogy and a corrupting force in popular democracy.

The circumstances of the United States are such that in the economic sphere we are pulling further and further ahead of most countries, and are taking our dividends increasingly in the form of trivialities. Many other countries are caught in an economic trap of poverty and ignorance so deep that there is only faint hope of escape. We have it in our power, with little sacrifice, to give them a fair fighting chance to improve their condition. In saying that we should do so, one need not be starry-eyed. One can be down-to-earth about the possibilities and practical-minded about the ways and means. But one cannot be neutral toward the consequences of hugging all our mounting prosperity to our own breasts. Unless animated by the right spirit and administered with a view to moral obligations, there is a better chance that it will corrupt and demean us than the contrary. To what extent, even with the most exemplary behavior on our part, other countries could improve their situation cannot be foreseen. This depends upon their capacity to take advantage of opportunities. While we have a stake in this problem, it is primarily theirs.

During the past year or two, the facts and potentialities of foreign aid programs, and the principles by which they should be governed, have been undergoing a searching examination by men of intelligence and goodwill in a variety of public and private agencies. Since they necessarily have an eye on political exigencies, their reports are mainly oriented to the short run and geared to the relation between aid and national security. They are concerned with the amounts of aid, selectivity among recipients, capacity to utilize aid, administration, and other mundane short-run matters. But showing through most of them is a recognition, usually only implicit, that the responsibilities of the United States should be based on some higher, more fundamental and more permanent principle than national security.

The higher principle is necessarily a moral principle. If the sentiment of fear, which has heretofore provided the popular appeal of aid programs, is downgraded as an inadequate, though not an invalid, basis, some sentiment of obligation must supplement it. Such a sentiment is the natural outgrowth of the Christian heritage which, apart from any doctrinal commitment or ecclesiastical establishment, asserts a profound respect for the worth and dignity of the individual person and the principle of mutual assistance. It is a heritage which cannot be limited to the boundaries of national states and has applications to states as well as to individuals. As Lewis Mumford says, we require "a higher trajectory for life as a whole," supranational in character.

Foreign aid is an economic problem. It is also a political problem. But finally it is a moral problem. The moral imperative specifies no particular amounts, recipients or methods of aid. These will be subject to a variety of exigencies and to unavoidable compromises of political or military expediency. But it does dictate the spirit in which the problem should be approached. Lacking this spirit the potential role of the United States in establishing the higher trajectory will be severely limited, if not wholly aborted. Given the present low starting point of American public opinion, the first task is to cultivate the spirit. In this task, at the outset it may be defensible to practice a little political chicanery by advancing a moral purpose under the cloak of a security need, as already appears to be happening. But if the moral basis is not in the end recognized and respected, the damage to the destinies of other peoples will be matched by a deterioration of our own social life.

When moral principles are invoked in a consideration of economic policy, we inevitably find ourselves in rough and forbidding territory. The roughest territory of all in the international field is that of immigration policy. Here, more than anywhere else, tribal attitudes make their last stand. I cannot bring myself to argue that this is wholly wrong. There is, I think, "something of value" which would be undermined by an open policy. But it is necessary to admit that the defense of foreign aid may in part reflect a troubled conscience on this point.

STATEMENT ON BEHALF OF
THE NATIONAL COUNCIL OF
CHURCHES OF CHRIST
IN THE U.S.A.*

WALDO CHAMBERLIN

WALDO CHAMBERLIN *is Washington representative of the National Council of Churches of Christ in the U.S.A.*

. . . The National Council of Churches believes it has a responsibility to adopt and make known a position on foreign economic policy including mutual aid and trade. The achievement or failure to achieve the great Christian goals of dignity and worth of the individual, the brotherhood of man, and world peace is dependent not only on the behavior of each of us as individuals but also on group action, including governmental policy, which is therefore a matter of Christian concern.

Governmental policy in mutual aid and trade has an important bearing on the relations and well-being of people and of nations. What happens to people and nations and the world community because of the economic facts of life are matters of concern for religious faith and values. In such matters the churches have a particular interest and competence.

THE CHURCHES' EXPERIENCE AND COMPETENCE IN MUTUAL
AID THROUGH MISSIONS

First, the churches have long centuries of experience in working around the world helping people to help themselves in practical ways. In mission work, the churches pioneered in technical assistance and economic aid. They developed programs of education, literacy, literature, medicine, public health, agriculture, industry, communications, and leadership training. Today, churches working through our Division of Foreign Missions, by voluntary contribu-

* Reprinted from U.S. Senate Committee on Foreign Relations, *Hearings, The Mutual Security Act of 1958,* 85th Congress, 2nd Session, 1958, pp. 656-661.

tions of over $40 millions per year, support over 10,000 workers, who cooperate with more tens of thousands of trained nationals in over 50 countries. They continue to carry on expanding programs in schools, colleges, universities, training centers, agricultural stations, farms, shops, clinics, and hospitals.

CHURCHES SEE URGENT NEED FOR PUBLIC AS WELL AS PRIVATE PROGRAMS

Out of such long, fruitful, widespread experience and observation, the churches have reached the conclusion that there is an urgent, continuing need for voluntary and private programs, and the churches are, in fact, increasing their efforts in this field. We are convinced, also, that there is urgent need at this time for our Nation to develop public programs of mutual aid to greater scope and magnitude, expanded to the extent of our national capabilities but limited obviously by the capacities of the underdeveloped areas to utilize and absorb them.

RELIGIOUS AND MORAL FOUNDATIONS FOR CONSTRUCTIVE MUTUAL AID

The competence of the churches to speak on religious and moral questions is well established. It is on these grounds that we primarily base our support for constructive mutual aid. In mutual aid we are dealing ultimately with immediate questions of life and death and long-time questions of the nature of man and his destiny. These are moral and religious questions which rest on theology and religious faith.

While having a basic concern for the religious and moral issues, the churches recognize some of the so-called practical arguments for mutual aid, which also have certain moral values and issues involved in them: One is that mutual aid is essential in the struggle between freedom and Communist tyranny, to help the newer and less-developed nations to maintain their independence with growing stability and liberty. A second practical argument for mutual aid is the military one, to help support other nations in collective security. Most church people would support programs for collective security, but we hold that military programs and defense support cannot by themselves develop peace, and that indeed an overemphasis on them can endanger peace. Peace is jeopardized when military might is exalted at the expense of constructive programs in economic, political, ideological, and moral terms. A third practical argument for constructive mutual aid is that it is good business both for others and for ourselves in the present and in the long run. In this time of economic difficulties in our Nation, a good case can be made not only for maintaining but even increasing our mutual aid programs since about 75 percent of these funds go into the pockets of business and people in our country. The offshore purchases should be continued because they supply dollars which pay for our exports, and export employment here is essential to recovery.

I am certainly in favor of the economic aspects which support foreign aid, but I am speaking today for the churches and I am proud, not reluctant, to emphasize some basic religious and moral foundations which compel us as a Nation to greater responsibility in constructive mutual aid programs.

1. Humanity is indivisible; we are all interdependent under one God, Creator of us all.

2. Our stewardship as a wealthy nation in a world of poverty compels us to share in more adequate programs of mutual aid.

3. Another principle of moral and spiritual truth in mutual aid is this: When men and nations do not have real concern for the lives of others in need, they follow the ways of decline and death; when they do care for others they follow the ways of life and mutual well-being.

4. We believe human life is sacred, being of primary value, so mutual aid is indispensable as it literally makes the difference between life and death for some people, and improves living for millions of others.

5. In mutual aid we actually go beyond the material realities, to the things of the spirit and a witness to our basic values in the method and amounts we share in such programs.

The breakup of the Athenian alliance 2,300 years ago, in that extraordinary Greek nation that is one major source of our civilization today, was at no time [the result of] outside Persian or Macedonian power, but was internal because of its abandonment of mutual aid with its spiritual foundations.

MORAL CONCERNS AND NATIONAL SELF-INTEREST COMPLEMENT EACH OTHER IN CONSTRUCTIVE MUTUAL AID

In constructive mutual aid, the practical and the moral are not in conflict but in agreement; realism and Christian idealism meet in accord, self-interest and altruism are joined. From the perspective of religion and morality, we believe that our national self-interest at this moment of history is best fulfilled in recognizing that our destiny is inescapably bound with the destiny of the world. . . .

STATEMENT ON BEHALF OF
THE FRIENDS COMMITTEE ON
NATIONAL LEGISLATION*

EDWARD F. SNYDER

EDWARD F. SNYDER *is the Legislative Secretary of the Friends Committee on National Legislation.*

Programs Supported by Friends Committee: We strongly support nonmilitary economic aid, the Development Loan Fund, technical assistance through the United States program, the U.N. program, and the Organization of American States. We support the refugee assistance programs in Europe, the Middle East, Korea, Hong Kong, and elsewhere, the U.N. Children's Fund, malaria eradication, Atoms for Peace, and payment of ocean freight on relief shipments by voluntary agencies.

It is perhaps safe to say that, taken together, these programs represent the most constructive, enlightened, and humanitarian aspect of United States foreign policy. Our national concern for the well-being of people in other lands is clearly indicated here. The direct relationship between the well-being and security of others and our own is clearly recognized. Yet the cost of these programs is modest compared with other expenditures. They account for perhaps a quarter of the total funds requested for the mutual security program. Last year their cost was less than 3 percent of all military spending, and less than 2 percent of total Federal appropriations.

* Reprinted from U.S. Senate Committee on Foreign Relations, *Hearings, The Mutual Security Act of 1958,* 85th Congress, 2nd Session, 1958, pp. 662-664.

Removing Economic Development Programs from Cold War Arena: In addition to expressing our strong support for the non-military programs in the mutual security bill, I wish to stress related subjects—the basic motivation for the mutual security program and support for the United Nations programs.

1. World economic development should be taken out of the cold war among nations and encouraged as a positive program for people.

Our government officials say that the Sino-Soviet bloc has extended about $2 billion in credits and grants for economic and military aid to other nations over the last 3 years. The dominant theme being used by the administration to persuade the Congress and the American public to accept the mutual security program is that the cold war has now shifted from the military to the economic field and the United States must be ready to match the Soviet Union loan for loan and grant for grant. Competition in the economic sphere is infinitely to be preferred to competition in the development of weapons of mass destruction. Yet the need for economic development of all countries would be just as great if communism never existed.

There are important disadvantages in treating economic development programs as a tool in the cold war: The desirability of projects and their relative priority tends to be determined more by political and military factors than by economic and social considerations. Attempts by underdeveloped nations to play off the great powers against each other create an unhealthy situation for all parties concerned. International tension is increased when economic development becomes a divisive influence. This is especially unfortunate in those many areas where cooperation among nations in a region is essential to adequate economic development.

We plead for leadership by the Foreign Relations Committee, the Congress, and the administration to take economic development out of the cold-war context and find a new and sounder rationale. We must recognize the increasing interdependence of all men on our shrinking planet. Economic and technical assistance programs should arise from a concern for the welfare of every individual in every part of the world, recognizing that our Nation's future well-being is intimately bound up with the well-being of all.

United States policy should be designed to help that part of the human race, about two-thirds of whom are sick or illiterate or politically or economically disadvantaged, develop their God-given potentialities. It means primarily helping others help themselves to do the things they want to do toward our joint community aspirations and ideals. This kind of program must express both a deep, passionate concern for people and a determination that they need not suffer from conditions which are not their fault. We should settle into this task on a long-range basis.

Channelling Assistance Through the United Nations: The United Nations today offers the major opportunity to take world economic development out of the cold war. Devoted to peace and representing 82 nations in the international community, it has the confidence of the world's people and the integrity to undertake such a program. As yet it has only a modest technical assistance program and no real economic development program at all, since the United States and several other nations which would undoubtedly be major contributors have hesitated to support the chief proposal in this area for a Special United Nations Fund for Economic Development.

We suggest that, at a time when United States leadership in foreign affairs is sorely needed, a major contribution could be made if the United States would announce its intention to channel most of its economic and technical assistance through the U.N. and challenge the Soviet Union to do the same.

THE INTERNATIONAL DILEMMA*

SPRUILLE BRADEN

SPRUILLE BRADEN, *former United States Ambassador to Argentina, is the author of numerous criticisms of United States foreign economic policy.*

. . . But enough of the past. Instead, I shall list just a few of our present sins and sentimentalities which, since their inception, have grown into serious threats to our security. Fortunately, it still is not too late to wipe them out and so strengthen ourselves both at home and abroad.

Both Democratic and Republican administrations have made peace almost the sole objective for their foreign policies. Of course, we want peace. But I submit that honor and honesty, freedom and decency, self-respect and respect of others are infinitely more important.

There is no sense, at the summit or anywhere else, in talking about peace or coexistence with Communist governments. They may squabble a bit amongst themselves, but every one of them is dedicated to the annihilation of both our faith and our Nation.

They will stop at nothing to enslave and debauch mankind. Unless we act on these cold facts, they will bury us as Khrushchev prophesied. Either we destroy communism, or it will destroy us.

Let us cut out the sentimental farce of cultural, agricultural or scientific and other interchanges with Communist-controlled nations. They, and not we, will benefit. Also, by thus lending prestige to the Communists, we set a bad example, which others follow.

It is a mortal sin to tolerate Communists anywhere. But above all, it is a sin to tolerate them in our Government. Witness the statement by Lt. General Trudeau, the Army's Chief of Research and formerly of Intelligence, that the Soviet's rapid military advances reflected successful espionage within the United States, rather than scientific prowess within the U.S.S.R.

It is only a somewhat lesser sin to allow in critical government and civilian posts socialists, well-intentioned idealists, unidentifiable theys, and others who too often are ready dupes for the Com-

* Reprinted from "The International Dilemma" by Spruille Braden, *U.S. Congressional Record*, 86th Congress, 1st Session, 1959, pp. A2220-2222.

munists. The career Foreign Service, as I have known it so intimately, by and large was a fine body of trained and competent diplomats. Unfortunately, the Service has been submerged by swarms—literally thousands—of outsiders brought into the State Department, the International Cooperation Administration (ICA), and other Government offices. Probably a majority of these are loyal citizens, but some just do not know the traditions and real meaning of the United States. A few of these, having risen to policy making or influencing posts, often speak for the State Department, and so can and do distort or ignore those basic precepts by which this Nation has been guided until recent years.

We have helped communism, the anti-Christ, by giving billions to Tito and Gomulka, and encouraged and financed socialism elsewhere.

Since 1940, the forces laboring to get Uncle Sam to give away everything he has, have grown extraordinarily effective. Some of our World War II giveaway may have been essential, but others, as in Latin America, were silly and useless. Then came UNRRA; we put up the money, but Stalin and Tito got the thanks. After 1946, help had to be given on a so-called temporary basis to devastated Europe—yet we are still giving. Later we said our aid was to defeat communism, although we had invited the Soviet to be a beneficiary of the Marshall Plan. Now, the sentimentalism is advanced that morally we are obligated, as a matter of Christian charity, to help the underdeveloped nations industrialize and raise living standards at a speed, anyone with a speck of common sense knows is unattainable.

Egging us on in this quixotic misadventure are the Communists, abetted by Socialists and do-gooders, plus thousands of bureaucrats, anxious to continue a luxurious living to which they fast are becoming accustomed.

From the start, proposals were advanced for the U.S. Government to finance equity investments and make increasingly soft loans. One official committee after another advocated these global giveaways. A rear guard action against these programs has been fought by U.S. investors, assisted by the still sound managements of the International (World) and Export-Import Banks. At least a show of businesslike procedures and protection of private property had been retained until lately.

Now, the defense is weakening. Inevitably, 12 years of government-to-government loans and grants have eroded the resistance and common sense of both the executive and Congress. Many private business leaders either are uninformed or subjected to the strongest kind of political and other pressures. Some accept each successive step as an alternative to something worse. Valuable contracts are offered by ICA as enticements to both employers and labor leaders.

The Development Loan Fund has been formed to make soft loans payable in local currencies, with which already we are surfeited. These loans are so dubious that no existing private or official institution would be allowed to make them. In addition, there are plans for similar funds in the Middle East and Latin America, to which we would be the main contributor, but without management control. Under Gresham's law, these bad credits will drive out the good, with dire consequences for both lender and borrowers. This is confirmed by the Fairless committee appointed by the President to study foreign aid. It said this type of loan was "undesirable and should be terminated."

From the outset, these Statists, Socialists, and Communists have tried to set up these programs in the United Nations under their control but with Uncle Sam footing the bills. For a time, SUNFED (Special United Nations Fund for Economic Development) was blocked. But the victory was short-lived. The trend is toward U.N. control. President Eisenhower has suggested the organization of an International Development Association as a soft loan affiliate of the International Bank and Secretary Dulles declared at the U.N. Assembly opening: "We propose that the nations dedicate the year 1959 to these purposes of economic development."

A continuation of our vast giveaways will be disastrous, but with the U.N. Communists and Socialists, neutralists, and suppliants for aid more and more directing the spending of your and my money, world ruin through inflation and bankruptcy will become inevitable. There will be no incentive for countries to put their houses in order and balance their budgets, stop inflation, and create favorable environments to attract private investment. Poverty, dissatisfaction and socialism will spread, while we in the United States will face ever bigger deficits and taxes and an ever smaller dollar.

This alarming and tragic outlook readily can be reversed by returning to the provenly successful methods of private enterprise, which have brought far greater and more widespread benefits to everyone concerned than governments ever could. I know firsthand what magnificent jobs have been done by the great mining and other companies throughout Latin America, including your own Boston-born United Fruit Co., which has performed miracles, converting uninhabitable jungles and swamps into valuable farmlands and raising the standard of living.

Those who beg for aid should remember how an undeveloped New England became a rich center of industry and finance. It was not by loans or grants from abroad, nor even because of its own natural resources. It was by courage and character, the initiative and moral qualities of its sturdy citizens. The great economist, Luigi Einaudi, former President of Italy, made this clear when he wrote:

"The heart of American wealth has not been in the rich Southern cotton regions, in the fruitful middle western plains, in the coal, iron, or oil regions. It lay in the New England States, in the inhospitable stony regions between New York and the Canadian border where the land yields little because of the profusion of rocks, where even the forest grows with difficulty, where there are no minerals of any kind, indeed where everything is lacking except the indomitable energy of man."

The only sensible thing, the Christian thing for us to do, is to give the indomitable energy of man a chance to work.

"Love thy neighbor as thyself" implies that a rational love of self is the basic standard measure, and gage which must guide us. Charity does begin at home in our Christian-Judaic religions.

One should neither sin or bankrupt himself for the sake of his neighbor, however pressing the latter's needs may be. The head of the family's duty is not to engage in futile sentimentality but first to care for his own, however pitiful may be the appeals for charity or help from others.

In our times, the future of all civilization hangs upon the integrity and security, solvency, and prosperity of the United States. If, through the continued and growing abuses of foreign aid, we bleed to death, liberty, order and peace, will be extinguished everywhere.

I pray that we start solving our problems at their beginnings and that soon we purge ourselves of the sins of both omission and commission and of the sentimentalities, so barren of real moral content, which now plague us. I pray that we quickly return to the honesty, realism, and high principles of the Founding Fathers, the courage of the minutemen, and respecting ourselves, demand and merit respect from all others. Truly, there is no other road to survival.

V

The National Interest as the Goal of Foreign Aid: Security–the Primary Objective

About the Readings

The major concern of this section is to examine foreign aid as a device to promote the national interest of the United States. "National interest" is a very ambiguous term and the reader is cautioned to search carefully for its meaning in the context of the various articles. The reader should note that many of the articles in this and the following sections are based on the assumption that the main goal of foreign policy is the protection of the "security" of the United States. In this connection, he should also note that there are several different interpretations of what "security" implies.

The first article, by Edward S. Mason, attempts a comprehensive survey of the objectives of United States foreign-aid activities and reaches a definite conclusion about the nature, desirability, and focus of our aid activities. The author is generally counted among

*the supporters of foreign aid, but he makes some significant quali-
fications.*

*James R. Schlesinger's article, "Foreign Aid: A Plea for Real-
ism," brings into question some of the contentions and claims in
Professor Mason's article. What different interpretation of security
does he have? What relationships between security and economic
development does Professor Schlesinger indicate? What does he
offer as "realistic criticism" of the scope and purpose of the foreign-
aid program? What proposal does he make for the proper focus of
our aid activities?*

*(For another point of view concerning the relationship between
realism and idealism, the reader is referred to Thomas I. Cook and
Malcolm C. Moos,* Power Through Purpose: The Realism of
Idealism as a Basis for Foreign Policy *[Baltimore: Johns Hopkins
Press, 1954].)*

UNITED STATES INTERESTS IN
FOREIGN ECONOMIC
ASSISTANCE*

EDWARD S. MASON

EDWARD S. MASON, *Dean of the Graduate School and Professor
of Economics at Harvard University, has been a member of
the President's Committee on Foreign Aid, deputy to the
President's Special Assistant on Foreign Economic Policy, and
is a frequent contributor to various periodicals.*

THE HUMANITARIAN FACTOR

An attempt to reassess the nature of United States interests is
the more important because there appears to be in recent discussion
a great deal of confusion concerning the sources of humanitarian

* Reprinted from *International Stability and Progress,* The American
Assembly, 1957, pp. 63-91.

contributions and the relative magnitude of our economic and security interests. The chief sources of confusion seem to be the following:

1. A failure to distinguish between, on the one hand, the motivations of American citizens and private institutions concerning foreign assistance and, on the other, the considerations that will lead the government to take actions that, over time, will be supported by American taxpayers and the electorate.

2. A false identification of our security interests with purely military considerations.

3. An exaggerated assessment of our present or future dependence on foreign sources of raw materials or on foreign markets.

The generosity of American citizens and private institutions in the foreign field is legendary. At an earlier period the motivation might have been largely religious; in this century it appears to be almost entirely humanitarian. The results of this generosity are impressive. Roberts College in Istanbul and the American Universities at Beirut and Cairo bear testimony to the magnitude and success of American educational effort in the Middle East. The Ford Foundation contributions in the Middle East and Southern Asia, which currently total about $15 million a year, are larger than the contributions in this area of a number of Colombo Plan countries. The health and agricultural programs of the Rockefeller Foundation in Latin America and elsewhere have substantially improved living conditions in many countries. Those are but a few examples.

There is, moreover, little doubt that the motivations that have led private citizens abroad to assist in promoting the welfare of depressed populations are similar to those that lead many people into United States government service in technical and other foreign aid programs. Furthermore, it is difficult to explain certain actions of the government in the foreign field—the Point Four Program may be an example—except on the basis of humanitarian considerations. This has been an element in a much broader range of foreign aid actions since the war.

Despite all this it is doubtful that humanitarianism (a desire to improve the living conditions and opportunities of people abroad without regard to the security or economic prosperity of the United States) can be considered important either in explaining the actions of this country since 1947 or in laying the basis for a reasonable expectation of future action. Government aid programs are devised and promoted in an administrative and political setting that is not very amenable to humanitarian considerations. The agencies of government responsible for the initiation and administration of these programs have annually to justify them before a Congress concerned with demonstrating to its voting constituencies that their interests are being served. An administration unable to show that taxes for foreign aid programs have some fairly direct relation to the economic interests of important political groups or to the safety of the State will have difficulty in continuing these programs—and, probably, continuing in power.

It seems necessary to labor this point because in many quarters there appear to be expectations that a sizeable international program of assistance, particularly from the United States, can be established without regard to the economic and security interests of the contributing countries. These expectations are set forth most explicitly perhaps by Gunnar Myrdal, Executive Secretary of the United Nations Economic Commission for Europe, in his recent book *An International Economy*. Myrdal's argument simply put is:

> That in the "integrated" societies of the West there has been taking place over the last century, largely because of a revolution in moral ideas, a redistribution of income and an equalization of opportunity. The effect has been that most citizens have acquired a sense of participation in their society that has largely eliminated the significance of earlier class struggles.
>
> That an "integrated" international society requires a similar redistribution of wealth and income and of economic opportunity between the rich and economically developed economies of the West and the so-called underdeveloped areas of the world.
>
> That there is substantial evidence of a spread of the ideas and values necessary to bring this about.

It is no doubt true that in the economically developed societies of the West redistribution of income and equalization of economic opportunity have gone far and have contributed greatly to social cohesion. According to Myrdal

> This process has . . . been determined largely by the ideal—a living force in the minds of these nations—of achieving an ever-greater equality of opportunity for all their citizens. One of the most important of state interventions in the nationally integrated economies has been the increasing application of the principle of sharing burdens. The

readiness to share displayed by the various groups comprising the nation state has been an index of the strength of the psychological basis for integration.

Without questioning the change in moral ideas over the last century or what constitutes a "just" distribution of income and economic opportunities, it is pertinent to remark that the redistribution was greatly facilitated by the shift in political power made possible by the spread of democratic practices and institutions. On the international scene there is no political structure within which a shift of power from the "haves" to the "have nots" can take place.

This being so, is it likely that changing attitudes toward burden-sharing and equalization of opportunities will, by their own strength, lead to international channeling of economic assistance from developed to underdeveloped countries?

Myrdal's argument that they will—or at least may—depends partly on what seems to be a misreading of the motives of our post-war aid programs. Of the Marshall Plan he writes, "It does not require any comprehensive or deep study of the American motives for this extraordinary aid to say from first-hand observation of the American people that, in the beginning, the main attitude was much more the positive one of sympathy and solidarity, rather than the negative one of fear of communism."

Myrdal goes on to say

> It is true that the Americans tried eagerly to convince themselves at the very inauguration of the Marshall Plan that they were acting solely with their own national interest in view, but this was only a further example of the strange suspicion on the part of the American people of their own generous motives, which I once analyzed as a slightly perverted element of their Puritan tradition.

Flattering as this view of American generosity may be, it does an acute disservice to anyone in the United States or in the underdeveloped areas who is attempting soberly to assess the conditions on which United States economic assistance is likely to be forthcoming.

Professor Jacob Viner, in "The Role of the United States in the World Economy," says

> The only factor which could persuade us to undertake a really large program of economic aid to the underdeveloped countries would be the decision that the friendship and alliance of those countries are strategically, politically, and psychologically valuable to us in the

cold war, that economic aid on a large scale can be relied upon to assure such friendship and alliance to us, and that the cost to us of a greatly enlarged program of economic aid would not be an excessive price to pay for these strategic gains.

Myrdal objects that "in the United States itself, this hardboiled policy which is so definitely out of line with the cherished humanitarian traditions of the nation, will not be an inspiring one." And, he goes on, "I personally doubt very much whether a comprehensive and lasting policy of international aid on a strategic basis will ever have a chance of becoming accepted in the United States."

It is here suggested, on the contrary, that the size and duration of a policy of international aid depends much more on the strategic situation than on anything else.

The report of the Commission on Foreign Economic Policy (Randall Report) states that "Underdeveloped areas are claiming a right to economic aid from the United States. . . . We recognize no such right." Myrdal characterizes this statement as "harsh." It is indeed harsh—and somewhat inexact. Some part of our postwar aid to underdeveloped areas has undoubtedly been motivated by a recognition of our "obligations" and of their "rights." But as a statement of American unwillingness to recognize any moral imperative to a large and sustained effort toward the economic development of underdeveloped areas, it seems substantially correct.

THE ECONOMIC FACTOR

We turn now to promotion of the economic interests of the United States as a possible explanation of postwar foreign assistance programs. There can be no doubt that, with respect to the Marshall Plan at least, this was an important motivating force. The United States participated during and immediately after the war in the development of policies and institutions designed to reestablish the network of world trade and international payments on a less discriminatory and freer basis than had existed just before the war. These policies and institutions contributed to the economic interests of the United States—and all trading nations. It became clear, however, early in the postwar period that the "Bretton Woods" policies and institutions were not going to work unless and until the trade and payments positions of Western European countries were brought into better balance than the devastation of the war permitted. One of the important objectives of the Marshall Plan was undoubtedly to bring this about.

Our continued concern with reducing trade barriers, currency convertibility, and nondiscrimination has probably facilitated Congressional acceptance of other foreign aid programs designed primarily for security purposes. Furthermore, the persistence of our foreign aid at the current level of $4 to $5 billion a year has come to be one of the pillars of a world trading system which, despite many barriers, is still much freer than the pre-war system. The contribution to our economic interest in multilateral, nondiscriminatory trade has been, in a sense, an extra dividend from foreign assistance designed primarily to accomplish security objectives.

Assigning full value to these economic considerations, it is, nevertheless, obvious that we would never have put $50 billion into foreign aid programs during the last ten years if our primary objective had simply been the promotion of our own economic welfare. The costs would have been judged too flagrantly disproportionate to the possible benefits. Our dependence on foreign trade is not such as to make even a substantial curtailment of trading relations a serious obstacle to economic growth and prosperity.

If we now consider prospectively the economic case for foreign assistance programs, particularly to underdeveloped areas, the following arguments are frequently pressed:

1. It is said to be impossible for the United States to prosper indefinitely in a world in which half the population continues to be ill-fed and ill-clothed.

2. Our increasing dependence on foreign sources of raw materials will necessitate an increased concern with the economic development of raw-material-producing areas if we expect to continue drawing supplies from these areas.

3. We shall encounter increasing difficulty in maintaining full employment in the United States unless we develop export markets through foreign lending or through foreign aid programs.

None of these arguments can withstand careful analysis. The economic growth of the United States over the last century took place in a world in which more than half the population continued to live at subsistence level. This fact suggests that rising levels of income elsewhere are not a necessary condition to our prosperity. Since the war our total imports have averaged between 3 and 4 per cent of gross national product. Our somewhat higher exports are explained by extraordinary United States aid programs. This small degree of dependence on foreign trade suggests a substantial insulation of American economic welfare from economic conditions outside our borders. It can be admitted that economic conditions in the underdeveloped areas of the world may have political consequences endangering world peace. But then the argument for concerning ourselves with the conditions of others becomes a political-security argument to which we shall turn presently. If one concentrates on economic relationships alone, the facts seem to be that although rising incomes in underdeveloped areas may, on balance, be economically beneficial to the United States, our national income can continue to expand at traditional rates in the absence of such an increase.

Raw material supplies. The raw material position of the United States is changing substantially. Before the war we were net exporters of raw materials on a substantial scale. Since the war, while we have consumed roughly 50 per cent of the industrial raw material output of the free world, we have produced only 45 per cent. In 1950, as the Paley Commission observed, we imported net about 9 per cent of our total consumption of industrial raw materials and unprocessed foodstuffs. On the basis of unchanged international trade policies, the Commission estimated that we might be importing 20 per cent of our expected consumption by 1975.

Does this projected increase in our dependence on foreign raw material argue for increased support of general economic development in underdeveloped areas? It does so only if it can be shown (a) that the availability of raw materials from abroad is closely connected with the rate of over-all economic development in resource countries and (b) that a curtailment of foreign sources of raw material supply would substantially hamper the economic growth of the United States. Neither position can be plausibly defended.

The overwhelmingly important current and prospective sources of our raw material imports are the Western Hemisphere and Africa south of the Equator. In the Western Hemisphere the countries from which we mainly import are already undergoing a process of economic development substantially independent of United States governmental assistance other than largely commercial-type loans from the Export-Import Bank. In Africa south of the Equator United States assistance is probably not a condition of continued access to raw material supplies, though this situation could change.

It should be noted in this connection that while the Western Hemisphere and Africa south of the Equator are the important raw material sources, our foreign aid since the war has gone predominantly to Europe, the Far East, and Southern Asia.

In assessing the possible consequences of curtailment of raw material imports, it is important to be aware of some of the magnitudes involved. The value of all industrial raw material and unprocessed food supplies in the American economy is about 10 per cent of gross national product. Our imports of these materials constitute about 1 per cent of G.N.P. A substantial rise, therefore, in the price of these imports would have only a small effect in checking our economic growth. Furthermore, a substantial rise in import prices would lead, in the case of many important materials, to a substitution of domestic for foreign output. The American economy is relatively invulnerable to a curtailment of foreign sources of raw material supply. The same thing cannot be said of our European allies; but if a case is made for aid programs on the ground that otherwise Western European sources of supply will be endangered, this becomes a political or security rather than an economic argument.

One final point: since the war the extraordinary United States governmental expenditures abroad associated with raw materials have been concerned mainly with stock-piling and with the development of sources of supply of strategic materials. While these expenditures have frequently contributed to economic development in resource countries, the objective has clearly been American security.

Export markets and investment outlets. There is a view that full employment in the United States requires an excess of exports over imports, financed either by private capital exports or by government foreign aid programs. Since the war this view has been endemic in various underdeveloped areas of the world, particularly Southern Asia. It leads to the convenient conviction that over the long run the United States will be led by its own economic interests to finance the foreign exchange component of expanding development programs in these areas. If it is replied that, in the event of private savings outrunning private investment opportunities, there are plenty of outlets for public, domestic investment in highways, schools, land reclamation, urban renewal, and the like, it is argued that the volume of public investment required to sustain full employment will be impossible of attainment within the framework of the "capitalist system."

It is a little hard to take this version of the "stagnation thesis" seriously when the combination of public expenditures and private investment and consumption is leading us perilously close to serious inflation. But it is true that an important component of effective demand for labor in the United States since the war has been an annual export surplus of $4-5 billion together with defense expenditures much larger, relative to G.N.P., than before the war. It is at least arguable that, if a change in the world situation permitted a reduction of defense expenditures and of foreign aid programs based on security considerations, we might have an employment problem on our hands. And the American attitude toward exports is somewhat different from that of most industrial countries. In most countries exports are regarded as a means of paying for necessary imports. Here we have sometimes tended to regard them as a sustainer of employment.

Two things may be said about this thesis that our interests in sustaining employment will lead us into foreign aid programs to promote development abroad. First, there are currently no signs that the level of defense expenditures at home and abroad can safely be reduced. Second, if a reduction becomes possible and *if* the employment effects of such a reduction are not offset by increases in private investment and consumption, the opportunities for public investment within the framework of what might be called a "capitalist system" appear limitless. After all, as we have had occasion to see since 1932, the "capitalist system" comprises a fairly flexible set of institutions.

In sum, an appraisal of the "economic interests" thesis concerning our postwar foreign aid programs lead us to the view that we have here at best a very incomplete and partial explanation.

THE DOMINANT FACTOR—POLITICAL AND SECURITY INTERESTS

There remains the overwhelmingly important motivation of our major postwar lending and spending programs and the principal justification for sizeable future assistance—namely, the furtherance of the kind of world in which we can live and prosper under institutions chosen by and not for us. Our security interests, however, comprise a complex set of ends and means. Expressed negatively, the promotion of these interests does not necessarily mean the enhancing of our ability to make war. It does not necessarily involve an increase in military expenditures. And it has no necessary connection with the encouragement of anti-communist sentiments or activities. On the other hand it obviously may and can involve all these things.

Furthermore, the long-run security problem is by no means limited to our relations with the Soviet Union. Conflagrations may break out in the Middle East, Southern and Southeastern Asia. Whether or not the communist world is involved, these can be inimical to our interests. And, over time, the world has a way of changing. During the next decade or two the prospect is one of explosive change in Southern and Eastern Asia and in Africa, under the impact of rapid population growth, developing nationalism, and the application of western technologies to unexploited resources. When the power relations in the world a mere half-century ago are contrasted with the situation today, it requires no great imagination to envisage a world fifty years hence in which Africa and Asia, not to mention Latin America, will have assumed quite different dimensions. Since we are presumably going to have to exist in that world, it behooves us to take what steps we can to assure that we live under our own freely developing institutions and at peace with any new constellation.

United States security policy, then, includes measures to assure and perpetuate peace and to insure our defense if peace can not be attained. Obviously there may be conflicts between these ends and their appropriate means. In the search for peace we may be led to pursue measures such that if peace fails we will be ill prepared to defend ourselves. And in the search for increased strength we could be led to act in such a way as to make peace impossible. If, as Myrdal appears to think, something like an integrated international society could be achieved by the voluntary burden-sharing and equalization of opportunities to which he attributes the emergence of integrated national societies; and if this were demonstrably the only road to peace, we might find ourselves embarking on a security program in the exclusive form of large-scale aid to the development of underdeveloped areas. Whether this could be described as a security program or sheer humanitarianism invokes the old utilitarian dilemma of whether a man whose greatest happiness lies in serving others is or is not acting in his own interests.

It is not necessary, however, to solve this dilemma here. We can take the firm position that United States security necessitates military expenditures large enough for an effective defense. But we can still recognize that a purely economic foreign aid program, say in the Middle East, designed to lessen the chance of war in that area, may be an appropriate part of our security policy. . . .

A BROAD CONCEPT OF SECURITY INTERESTS

Since the Korean War, Congress has been reluctant to support foreign assistance not tied to a military formula. This is an excessively narrow conception of the means appropriate to the advancement of American security interests. Assistance has been denied to countries, like Ceylon, who traded with communist nations even though these nations offered the only feasible outlet for their products. Burma and Indonesia have been led to reject United States aid because of a belief they were being asked to take sides in the Cold War. If aid without strings might plausibly be expected to add to political stability, insistence on such strings has no place in a sensible security policy.

The reaction of those responsible for the conduct of United States foreign policy to recent events in Poland and Hungary is one indication that our interests abroad involve something more than mere anti-communism. Continued support for Tito is another. It may not be to our interests to encourage revolt against communism within the Soviet orbit if the inevitable crushing of these revolts is followed by a reversion to Stalinism in the affected area. On the other hand, an increasing degree of independence among European and Asian statellites, even though they continue to be communist, is to be encouraged.

Security policy, then, is concerned with maintaining peace as well as with assuring defense if peace cannot be maintained. The means appropriate to these ends are in no sense purely military. They do not inevitably involve a merely negative anti-communism. They require a high degree of discrimination in their use as among particular areas. If we recognize all this, we are in a better position to assess the merits of the development programs of underdeveloped areas in relation to a sensible United States security policy. . . .

THE CURRENT OUTLOOK ON THE SECURITY PROBLEM

Strategic Factors Predominant but Not Exclusive. Since 1950 the character of our foreign aid programs has continued under the influence of that diagnosis, even though it has become increasingly clear that in many respects the diagnosis is incomplete and inadequate. For a time it apeared to be our view that the Korean War had, or should have, made the world alignment of forces so abundantly clear that we were entitled to conclude that those who were not for us were against us. In attempting to attach political conditions to proffered aid programs we were rebuffed in Burma and Indonesia. India made it quite plain that an acceptance of economic aid would not affect her position of neutrality. The emphasis we attempted to place on restricting trade with Soviet-bloc countries further weakened our influence in Asia and, to some extent, in Europe. Since to our minds the dominant security consideration was the division between Soviet communism and the rest of the world, we constantly overestimated the unity of the "free world" and paid much too little attention to bitter and continuing sources of friction within it. The Baghdad Pact, regarded by us as a defensive alliance against possible Soviet aggression, was viewed in a different light in most of the Arab states. And the decision to extend military aid to Pakistan may have been taken with too little regard to repercussions in India and Afghanistan.

The over-simple, post-Korean diagnosis of the security threat has to some extent been corrected. We now recognize that neutralism is not necessarily inimical to United States interest and a bar to United States assistance. Certainly, from the point of view of our own security, it is better to support a position of neutrality in an important area than to see that area come under Soviet influence. We have also moderated to some extent our proscription against trading in strategic materials with iron-curtain countries. As one of the results, we now have a technical assistance mission in Ceylon. Nevertheless, as the following figures on foreign aid tend to indicate, the military threat diagnosis is overwhelmingly predominant.

Foreign Aid Appropriations F/Y 1957

Direct Military	$2,018,000,000
Defense Support	1,162,000,000
Economic development, technical aid and all other foreign assistance	625,000,000

. . . The limitations imposed by the present military situation on a reassessment of foreign aid programs can hardly be overlooked. Despite this fact there have been changes in the world that make the present security problem look different from that at the time of the Korean War. The first of these is the emergence of a possible shift in Soviet strategy and tactics away from military competition and the threat and practice of armed intervention toward what is commonly called a policy of competitive coexistence. A second is evidenced on both sides of the iron curtain by a certain loosening of ties that in the Soviet orbit had been forged by the policies of Stalin, and in the Free World were the inevitable reaction to the kind of threat that Stalinism represented. The third change is the emergence of China as a rapidly developing Asiatic power with an obvious role to play in any policy of competitive coexistence. . . .

ECONOMIC DEVELOPMENT IN UNDERDEVELOPED AREAS AS
A UNITED STATES SECURITY OBJECTIVE

The Relation of Security Interests to Economic Development. Our security interests properly include not only the maintenance of peace but the promotion of a world order in which if countries are not aligned with us they at least will not be aligned with our potential enemies. Despite the fact that our trade with South and Southeast Asia is small and the opportunities for mutually beneficial investment seem limited, what happens there concerns us deeply. The economies of South Asia may not be complementary with our own, but they are complementary with the economies of our Western European allies, and, increasingly, with the economy of the Soviet Union. Currently the exchange of European manufactures for the raw materials of South and Southeast Asia is a part of world trade on which our allies heavily depend. A large-scale shift in the economic relations of South and Southeast Asia from western Europe to the Soviet Union could have profound economic and political consequences.

From the purely strategic point of view the importance of Asian space presumably does not need to be argued. These are relatively short-run interests. But South and Southeast Asia now contain a quarter of the population of the world and may, with economic development, embrace a much larger share of the world's economic resources than now. In the longer run, therefore, our relations with that area could well become a matter of vital concern. Today we are primarily interested in the effects of developments in South and Southeast Asia on our relations with the Soviet powers. Tomorrow we may be confronted with a different alignment.

FOREIGN AID: A PLEA
FOR REALISM*

JAMES R. SCHLESINGER

JAMES R. SCHLESINGER, *Associate Professor of Economics at the University of Virginia, has been an academic consultant in economics at the Naval War College and is the author of* The Political Economy of National Security (*New York: Praeger, 1959*).

In the prevailing climate of opinion, it has become unfashionable to challenge the widespread supposition that the principal purpose of the mutual security program should be to spur economic growth in the less developed lands. Neither it is popular to raise questions concerning the extent of American capabilities to foster development. As a consequence of the concern over the future relations of the West with the newly emerging states of Asia and Africa, development assistance has been seized upon as the best answer, if not the only answer, to the problem of curbing the expansion of Sino-Soviet power into the affected areas.

Informed opinion appears to be virtually unanimous in support of the increasing emphasis upon economic assistance, as embodied in the President's most recent budget requests. One member of the Senate's Foreign Relations Committee has argued that the destiny of the world will be determined by what occurs in the underdeveloped nations of Asia. Last summer [1958] the Foreign Affairs Com-

* Reprinted from *The Virginia Quarterly Review*, Vol. 35 (Spring 1959), pp. 221-239. Copyright, 1959, by *The Virginia Quarterly Review*, The University of Virginia.

mittee of the House reported that curtailment of the assistance program "would immediately mean that we would lose the cold war." The Vice-president has stated that the nation can never be secure "as long as misery and poverty exist in any substantial manner in any part of the world." The Secretary of State [John Foster Dulles], who likes to frame political issues in theological terms, has observed that the program "is an expression of the moral law under which we live," and leaders of the Democratic Party have been inclined to chide the administration for doing too little rather than too much. Examples could be multiplied, all supporting the conclusion that the bulk of the nation's leaders accept the contention that the spurring of economic development is likely to provide security for the United States. In the 1958 State of the Union Message, the President summarized all the hopes that are held for the present program:

> The countries receiving this aid become bulwarks against Communist encroachment. . . . Nations that are conscious of the steady improvement in their industry, education, health, and standard of living are not apt to fall prey to the blandishment of Communist imperialists. . . .

Fundamentally the assistance program is a political issue: each observer's conclusions will depend upon his assessment of the non-economic factors involved. Economic analysis merely suggests that human wants are insatiable, and are limited only by the availability of resources. It therefore implies that the growing aspirations of the underdeveloped nations could not be satisfied even by a limitless flow of resources from the West. Poverty is a relative matter; with each increase in the standard of living, new desires and new dissatisfactions emerge. Even if there is such a thing as absolute poverty, however, the harsh reality is that the misery of half-starved, shelterless wretches cannot be eliminated in the foreseeable future. The expansion of income needed to raise living standards of the huge and burgeoning populations of the underdeveloped world to what we would regard as a tolerable level simply staggers the imagination. In view of the limited resources, the institutional barriers to advancement, and the population pressures, even assistance from the West more massive than has yet been contemplated would hardly permit *per capita* incomes to rise by more than 1 per cent or 1½ per cent *per annum*. Starting from so low a base, this would mean that at the end of a century the degree of poverty would still be appalling. . . .

Thus the stage is set for the "revolution of rising expectations," about which so much has been said in the literature on development assistance. It should have occasioned no surprise that when the possibility of improvement has been discerned man's desires would outrun his means. What is surprising about this age is the belief that the "rising expectations" might ever be satisfied, and that heaven could be achieved here on earth. In the nature of things, the rising expectations can never be satisfied, but the very fact that mankind has been encouraged to allow its hopes to outrun its capacity is a political condition with which we in the West must now reckon.

We should recognize, however, that we Americans bear a particular responsibility for these rising expectations. Fortunately situated as we have been, upon a virgin continent isolated from the penalties of war, we have fallen prey to the idea that evil men and outmoded institutions present the only barriers to rapid economic progress. We have gone around the world spreading the Gospel of Plenty, raising the level of expectations, cajoling skeptics into the need for higher aspirations. We have been unable to fight a war without formulating grandiose objectives. In the First World War, we fought to make the world safe for democracy. In the Second World War, in the message of the Four Freedoms, we added to the traditional democratic objectives of freedom of speech and religion, the unobtainable objectives of freedom from want and fear—in part, a simple extension to all mankind of the political attitudes engendered domestically by the depression of the thirties. Inevitably in the postwar world the hopes raised by these evanescent slogans have been deflated. Yet the effect of the slogans has lived on—and has been sustained by our words, so that the failure to realize the rising expectations is bound to be blamed upon America and the West. The United States is somehow responsible when the promise of easy progress goes unfulfilled.

It would seem most realistic to view the questions raised by Western relations with the newly emerging states as primarily political and psychological, and the economic element simply as the vehicle through which underlying sympathies or antipathies are expressed. It would be quixotic to assume that countries receiving aid or undergoing rapid economic development will necessarily become bulwarks against Communism. The future of the underdeveloped areas will be determined by the direction in which the peoples of these areas conceive their interests to lie, and it is perhaps the better part of wisdom to recognize that in many of these countries the attitude toward the West—conditioned as it is by past and present grievances, real and imaginary—varies only between ambivalence and hatred. To what extent this antipathy can be alleviated is problematical. Certainly economic aid, seen in the light of its very limited power to raise actual living standards and its not so limited power to raise illusory hopes, can alter the balance only in marginal cases. . . .

Political realism under these circumstances would impel us to admit what we cannot change, and to accept what we must endure. Instead, our uncertain relations in these emerging areas has led the West into a rather frantic frame of mind: we must not let them get away; we must do something. Our failure to recognize our limited capacity for affecting the dominant ideologies in the under-developed lands has made us all too receptive to the flood of dramatic advice that is heralded as the key to a Golden Age of international harmony—the rejection of which, it follows, will set us on the road to ruin. Such admonishments would seem to be a combination of both wishful thinking and romantic pessimism.

In all economic activities, advantages are mixed with compensating disadvantages; so also in the foreign aid program—a circumstance glossed over in recent discussions of the issue. On the one hand, it is true that benefits may accrue to the contributing power as a result of providing an increment of resources to the recipient power—through propaganda, a more effective military alliance, the possibility of good will engendered. But offsetting disadvantages often are more numerous and may make up in quantity what they lack of weight. The psychological reaction of the recipient is all important. All too frequently when aid is regularly conferred, it comes to be regarded as a right, and under the circumstances the recipient falls to brooding over the niggardliness of the allotment. In former colonial regions, this tendency is accentuated by the belief that the wealth of the West has been obtained by exploitation of the under-developed lands, so that any aid given by the United States may be viewed as vicarious atonement for injuries allegedly perpetrated by other Western powers. American aid may thus be construed as a guilt payment, and this likelihood is increased by the strange expressions of guilt on the part of some Americans that we are well-off in an impoverished world.

A second disadvantage stems from mutual jealousy among the

beneficiaries, who see no reason why others, possibly local rivals, should fare better at our hands than they do themselves. We have observed this factor in operation in terms of allies vs. neutrals, Pakistan vs. India, the Arab bloc vs. Israel, and Latin America vs. the nations of Europe, Asia and Africa.

Another disadvantage arises from the involvement of the contributing power in the affairs of the recipient states. One type of penalty is the responsibility for the success of programs over which the authority of the contributing power is, and properly should be, limited. Another penalty arises from the cultural clash between the administrators dispatched by the contributing power and the local inhabitants. The ways and the physical comforts to which Americans have grown accustomed, for example, cannot fail to excite resentment and envy among those whom we assist. We must recognize the shortage of suitable personnel in planning a program of assistance, and recognize that the costs of direct involvement may well be high. . . .

Many and varied have been the proposals advanced for the future direction of the aid program, with the majority envisaging an expansion of aid to the underdeveloped areas. Some have based the case for aid upon humanitarian motives; others suggest that the dispensing of aid is both a duty and a privilege, and for some, perhaps too heavily imbued with Marxist notions concerning the danger of substantial unemployment in the United States, it is more than a privilege, it is a necessity. These attitudes are too politically unrealistic to require much comment; the economic benefits of aid are too limited, the humanitarian motive is too frail to serve as the basis of a long-term program. The majority of the proposals, however, whatever their conclusions, are based upon what the proponents consider to be the long-term security interests of the United States.

These proposals cover the range of the political spectrum. At one pole is what might be called the free enterprise approach, rejecting all governmental economic assistance (although not necessarily military assistance) on the basis of ideological considerations. It is held that democracy can only flourish within the framework of a market economy and that by encouraging the growth of the governmental sector and of co-ordinated economic programs in other lands, we are fostering the growth of totalitarianism. In opposition it might be argued that it is unlikely either that the United

States could control the political orientation of other lands by refraining from aid, or that it would inevitably fail to find common international objectives with non-market economies. Consequently, "making the world safe for free enterprise" does not appear as a tenable political objective.

At the opposite pole is the suggestion that the United States, in concert with other Western nations, make available to the underdeveloped countries all of the economic assistance that they can profitably absorb "with no political strings attached." Such a program should not be designed to strengthen military capacity, to win friendship, or to strengthen private enterprise. Rather it is hoped that it will allay the unrest created by the disruption of traditional patterns and sustain the underdeveloped nations by providing an attractive vision of the future during the hard years ahead. It must be recognized, however, that political strings, no matter how loosely held, can never be eliminated from a long-term aid program, as the Yugoslavs have recently rediscovered. The costs of the program, moreover, in view of the free offer of aid, would rise astronomically as the absorptive capacity of the underdeveloped nations improved. Finally, the proponents themselves admit that based upon the economic possibilities alone, the picture is exceedingly bleak. Their program represents a calculated risk at long odds—essentially a long-term program which can hardly cope with our security problems, for the most part inherently short-run.

An intermediate and somewhat eclectic approach recognizes that the policy issues are many-sided, and not simply the promotion of economic development. Where military risks are substantial, military assistance should be extended. Rather than neglecting the "political strings" we should recognize that the search for a political settlement should constitute the heart of our program. It would be unwise, however, to concentrate exclusively on military assistance, because even limited economic assistance may serve to maintain political stability in regions where aspirations for economic development have become paramount. Although this eclectic approach may have exaggerated the degree to which Western aid can enhance Western security, it properly stresses the security aspect. A weakness, however, is that it has not set down firm guidelines for specific tactical decisions in the granting of aid.

It is a logical misfortune, but a practical necessity, that the amount and the allocation of foreign assistance must inevitably be based upon compromise between conflicting pressures, in which expediency as opposed to rules of policy will have some role to play. A policy framework, however, can be formulated within which the majority of specific issues may be judged as they arise. The first rule is a positive one: whenever we give aid, we must recognize and make use of its strategic implications, just as we should in the case of trade. In so far as they are related to foreign policy objectives, trade and aid should be viewed as equivalent and co-ordinate means to the same general end: to influence the international environment favorably to our own interests. This does not imply, of course, that whatever advances our interests must do so at the expense of others. The chief advantage of trade and of aid—the commercial weapons of strategy—is that they permit the conferring of mutual benefits, so that the interests of several nations may be served and co-ordinated by economic ties.

A corollary of this rule is recognition that of the two weapons, aid must generally be subordinate. Though assistance programs and trade are two methods of supplying foreign exchange, the former has drawbacks which the latter does not share. Assistance which implies dependency creates resentment between benefactor and beneficiary to a degree not characteristic of trade, which is less emotion-laden since it is part of the ordinary commercial routine. Trade relationships may be viewed as permanent, whereas aid must be viewed as a transitory phenomenon. In any quantitative appraisal, moreover, trade must loom much larger than aid. Probably until the day that hope succumbs to disillusionment, the American people will be willing to supply some funds for economic assistance, but in the nature of things these sums will not be large, for the taxpayers will insist that their interests be taken into account in the evaluation process.

Consequently, it may be argued that our policies have been moving in the wrong direction in recent years. We have encouraged expectations of aid which in the long run will not be forthcoming, and at the same time have been laggard in encouraging trade on which the main burden in the end must lie. The Eisenhower administration entered office using the slogan "trade not aid." It has resisted the pressure to return to high tariff policies, yet it has belied its lofty professions of adherence to liberalized trade by using restrictive devices other than the tariff to limit imports. In particular by imposing quotas upon oil importers and by forcing the Japanese "voluntarily" to limit their exports of textiles, china, and other items to this country, the administration has made it appear that "aid not trade" might well be a more appropriate epitaph to its foreign economic policies. In recent years the administration has endorsed the aid program with ever increasing vigor. But aid is inevitably a weak substitute for trade; it does not provide the permanency of trade ties, especially in view of its weak domestic political support. There can be little doubt that in the long run it would be advisable to rely increasingly upon the trade weapon.

It is important to recognize how restricted are the short-run economic possibilities in the underdeveloped areas, and how limited is the capacity of aid or of trade to alter those conditions. In this regard we must shed a number of romantic illusions. The more enthusiastic proponents of the aid program frequently assert that its goal is to reduce the gap between our living standards and those in the underdeveloped areas, thereby reducing envy and resentment of the West. Dr. Lewis Webster Jones, for example, in a recent report to the Senate on our assistance program in South Asia observed that "the gap between their poverty and our affluence is as obvious to them as it is to us; and the necessity for narrowing the gap is as important to us as it is to them." But the gap refuses to be narrowed; half a century from now it is likely to be greater than it is today. Even if the levels of living in underdeveloped areas were to double in the next generation, a most optimistic prediction, the absolute gap will increase as a result of the expected expansion of the advanced economies. When this unpalatable fact is mentioned to enthusiasts, they are likely to argue that perhaps the gap in living standards is not the important issue, but rather to spur industrial growth, or at least to make the attempt. This may be true, but it points to a certain degree of confusion over just what our objective in extending aid should be. Clarification of the purposes of the assistance program is essential, and we need to take care that there is some relationship between our objectives and the actual possibilities in the underdeveloped areas.

The amount of aid we can extend is limited; the task of development is herculean. Inevitably the problem of selection arises, and in the selection process two factors stand out. First, the limited capacity of aid to speed development should impel us to consider the propaganda and foreign policy aspects of the program as more important than development *per se*. Secondly, the greater the dispersion of the aid, the less will be its impact upon the economies of the recipients; the more concentrated, the more effective it will be. Even if we were to recognize fully the difficulties that stand in the way of development, the United States is likely to continue with the foreign aid program because of its implications for our international position—particularly in terms of its propagandistic value. But if the strategic aspects, rather than the developmental aspects, become paramount, we should recognize the implications.

This leads to a second proposal as a rule of policy which broaches the issue of neutralism: aid should be used in strengthening the international position of the West. Throughout the Cold War, the United States and other Western powers have sponsored regional military alliances to counter the threat of Communist expansion. Much criticism questioning the wisdom of such a policy has appeared, some of it penetrating, but as long as we rely upon such military arrangements, any aid program must support rather than weaken this instrument of foreign policy. Having given strong support to the broad policy objectives of the West, our military allies should never be treated in a fashion that conveys the impression that non-alignment, and even active opposition to Western policies, may frequently bring a nation greater rewards in terms of foreign aid. To cultivate such an impression is to provide an incentive for wholesale desertion from the Western camp.

It follows that whatever assistance we extend to the underdeveloped nations should be graduated in accordance with the support given Western policies and the degree of resistance to the policies of the Sino-Soviet bloc. That this is a harsh rule from the point of view of the Indians or the Cambodians cannot be denied, but they must accept the penalties, as well as the benefits, of their general foreign policy orientation. The argument that some of our military allies would make ineffective use of additional aid is misleading. The wasting of aid in itself is not relevant to the more fundamental question whether an allied power deserves more at the hands of the West than a state with a different orientation. Furthermore, it is doubtful whether the West should insist on its allies setting higher economic objectives. To encourage rising expectations and dissatisfaction with the prevailing degree of progress (or lack of progress) may simply further unsettle an already unsettled world.

As a power, the United States has been inclined to ignore its strong points in the attempt to shore up its position at its weakest—

hardly a judicious tactic if it leads to a weakening of the strong points. The maintenance of the political cohesion of the West—especially in our relations with Europe—should remain the primary consideration of American policy. Despite the existence of some antipathy toward the United States, the nations of Latin America have consistently given support to American policy and should never be given cause to believe that our treatment of them has been less satisfactory than that accorded less "reliable" countries. In Asia, our behavior has appeared on occasion to be something less than wise. It should not have been difficult to anticipate the reaction of the Baghdad Pact countries when, shortly after extending a $225 million loan to India, the United States promises to distribute $10 million among the pact members, as occurred in January, 1958. Such action suggests that alliance with the West does not pay. Unless the allocation of aid is closely correlated with our foreign policy objectives, the program will not represent even a calculated risk, but simply a miscalculation. Such an allocative procedure is supported by developmental considerations. Since aid is limited, it should be concentrated in a manner that will achieve maximum, long-run results. This would imply that Latin America should take precedence over Asia as an object of our attention. To rephrase the second rule: never should the aid program place a premium upon opposition to Western policies or neglect Western strong points.

There is an additional prescription which in the long run we would be well advised to follow. Financial irresponsibility ought not to be underwritten, with aid graduated either in accordance with the degree of recklessness of the recipient in handling its domestic affairs or in proportion to its ruthlessness in acquiring assistance. In other words, the amount of aid should be roughly predictable in advance, or else it may come to be regarded as a sort of expansible crutch useful for offsetting crippling domestic policies. If aid is determined by the size of the foreign exchange deficit or by the pace of inflation, a premium is placed upon the acceleration of the very spending that is the initial cause of the economic difficulties. Although a lenient attitude may be taken with respect to waste in the aid program, certainly the latter ought not to be organized in a way that provides an inducement for excessive expenditures.

On the basis of such considerations, the advisability of attempting to salvage India's current Five Year Plan, for example, is open to question, particularly with respect to its long-run implications. The Plan was overly ambitious, and it was so admitted from the first, but officials refused to reckon with the cold statistical facts since they held out insufficient hope for progress. The magnitude of the planned rupee and foreign exchange gaps was staggering, and in practice the original estimates proved to be too low. Expanded assistance now would mean that we place a premium upon overly ambitious (i.e., unrealistic) planning. Some observers have suggested that a most valuable lesson from this experience has been a trend toward greater realism among Indian planners. How wise is it to attack this new sense of realism by such assistance that embodies an implication that the United States is prepared to absorb the cost of reckless schemes? Not infrequently this issue is similarly posed by Latin American nations with chronic inflation and exchange problems. In the final analysis, it would seem advisable, despite the temptations, not to grant aid on the basis of simple expediency, since it encourages what might otherwise be temporary emergencies to become chronic.

It is impossible to develop any criterion for economic assistance which will not create dissatisfaction, since for almost all recipients the needs are insatiable and the only sound criterion is "more." Given the limited economic possibilities, we shall have to disabuse ourselves of romantic illusions concerning how much aid can accomplish beyond the propaganda field. The claims of realism may appear cheap and tawdry to those who would have us dedicate ourselves anew to the ideals of Woodrow Wilson, but in the end there is no alternative, and the costs of undiluted idealism generally run high.

VI

The Proper Means
of Foreign Aid:
Economic or Military

About the Readings

The focus of much of the remainder of this book is on the proper means for accomplishing foreign-aid objectives, a broad and complex subject deserving extensive analysis. Little more is done in this section than to suggest the main categories of argument and to illustrate some of the positions various influential people have taken. It should not be assumed that because an individual supports one means, one particular emphasis, he rejects all others. Although this may happen on occasion, it is generally not the rule. Moreover, since the authors of the following comments, almost without exception, can be categorized as supporters of foreign aid, the assumption is that some form of aid should be used to further American interests abroad. Whether the emphasis should be on assistance that is military or economic, private or public, technical or otherwise is thus the major question of this section.

The first comment in this section is taken from testimony given before the House Foreign Affairs Committee by Secretary of Defense Neil McElroy. Although he is probably not one who believes that the foreign-aid emphasis should be exclusively military, he nonethe-less made it abundantly clear how important he thinks the military aid is. Perhaps few aspects of the foreign-aid question have come under such unrelenting attack among supporters of foreign aid as the military focus that a significant portion of our aid has taken. What seems to be Secretary McElroy's main argument in support of his contention that, despite critics, the military part of the aid is indeed indispensable? Would one's position on the nature of the nuclear stalemate influence one's analysis of the validity of his argument? In what way does the concept of collective security influence the Secretary's analysis of what the United States is trying to do in supplying arms to other countries?

In a speech to the Georgetown School of Foreign Service, Chester Bowles argued that the military emphasis of our foreign-aid program needs a radical shift. What reasons did he advance to support his contention that economic aid will be more satisfactory? If, as he asserts, anti-communism should not be the main goal of foreign aid, what did he offer as an alternative?

THE ESSENTIALITY OF THE MILITARY ASSISTANCE PROGRAM*

NEIL McELROY

NEIL McELROY *was United States Secretary of Defense when this testimony was given.*

The Acting Secretary of State has already testified with respect to the important contribution the Mutual Security program makes to the furtherance of United States foreign policy objectives.

* U. S. House of Representatives, Committee on Foreign Affairs, Mutual Security Act of 1959, *Hearings,* 86th Congress, 1st Session, 1959, pp. 67-70.

My own remarks will, therefore, be directed to the military assistance program, and specifically to its essentiality as an integral part of our own national defense. As you know, the executive branch is requesting new obligational authority in the amount of $1.6 billion for this program in fiscal year 1960.

There can be no question about the objective of our defense program. It is to maintain a military position of such strength that first, no nation will attack us because he will know that we can inflict unacceptable damage on him in return and second, local situations of tension can be prevented from breaking into war or can be contained if military conflict does begin.

This means that we must have military strength not only on this continent, but in the whole periphery of the free world where aggression is apt to occur. It has been many years since we could regard our frontier as the coastline of this country. We have long recognized that the advance of international communism anywhere weakens the security not only of the free world but of the United States itself. Aggression must be stopped. Our defense is tied inevitably to the defense of the far-flung frontiers of the world. We can expect one probing action after another in which the Soviets or the Communist Chinese test our willingness and ability to resist. If the free world cannot stand up firmly to these probes when they are initiated, we may well be faced with a major conflict as the Communists, pressing ahead with their win-by-threat policy, make it imperative that at some point we meet the issue squarely.

It is most unlikely that the United States alone could hold all these varied fronts dispersed widely around the world. The concept of a strength created and maintained by joining the capabilities of ourselves and our allies is thus basic to our whole security program. If our allies do not remain strong, our whole security concept will need radical revision and the burden placed on our own resources will be immeasurably greater.

We are most fortunate in the fact that in most of the areas where international communism might seek expansion, there are countries which are friendly to us and look to us for leadership. These nations have the will to resist, and they have the manpower. In many cases they do not have the resources. Without assistance they cannot support military establishments adequate to defend themselves. If we do not buttress them with the resources they need, and help them with the training necessary to prepare them for modern warfare, they will succumb to communism either through military action or through the kind of civil disorder and deterioration on which communism thrives.

We cannot let this happen. Each Communist success is a new discouragement to those who would cast their lot our way, and a new source of vitality and momentum for the aggressors.

In my judgment it would be shortsighted indeed if this Nation spent over $40 billion on its own Military Establishment and then declined to spend the much smaller sums needed to maintain and modernize the forces of our allies which are essential to our whole defensive concept, and without which our own military expenditures would have to be enormously increased.

I recently was privileged, as I am sure several of the members of this committee have been, to see at first hand the operation of our military assistance program in a number of countries in the Far East and Southeast Asia. I wish every Member of Congress could visit countries like South Korea and see what can be done when the United States supplies its know-how and resources to a nation determined to put them to good use. This, as you all know, is an active front; guns are facing each other across a hot boundary line; troops in forward dugout positions are on continuous 24-hour alert. If the South Korean forces which join our own and other United Nations units in holding this front were not well trained and well supplied, we would either have to throw in far larger forces of our own or move out with the knowledge that South Korea would fall as another victim to Communist aggression.

A dramatic illustration of our program at work was given at Quemoy where Nationalist Chinese engaged Communist Chinese aircraft and shot them down at a ratio of 8 to 1. They used American equipment and American training—both were essential. If the Nationalist Chinese had not been ready to defend themselves, either Quemoy would have been lost or we would have found ourselves engaged in war with the aggressing Communist.

Five years ago South Vietnam was demoralized from the effects of a bitter war and hardly had the strength to provide even a minimum amount of its own protection. Today, with their own courage and energy, together with our assistance, the situation has improved tremendously. They are now able to maintain civil order at a time of possible future crisis; and while South Vietnam could not, of course, stand up against an attack backed by the Sino-Soviet forces, it could defend itself against an invading neighbor and hold the line long enough for the Western World to come to its aid.

A prime example of the value of our mutual assistance program, of course, is the role it has played in the development of NATO defenses. It is no exaggeration to say that the fact that there has been no aggression in Europe since NATO was formed in 1949 is due primarily to the strengthened military posture and sense of collective security engendered by the military assistance program. The stanch stand of our NATO allies with us on the Berlin situation over the past 3 months exemplifies NATO's cohesion and solidarity.

There are many other examples. They add up to a most impressive supplement to the total forces defending the free world.

Some measure of the magnitude is gained from noting that the ground forces of our allies comprise today over 5 million men; naval forces, 2,500 combat vessels; and air forces, about 30,000 aircraft, of which 14,000 are jet. One can see their importance, and the problem we would face if we had to meet these military requirements with our own forces.

I have emphasized the contributions which our allies make to the collective security—and therefore to our own security—in the form of military personnel and equipment. I could just as well emphasize the fact that without staunch and stable friends overseas we would not have the network of overseas bases which is so vital to our own military operations. Our Strategic Air Command is considerably strengthened by its ability to operate from advanced overseas bases. The operations of our Navy are greatly helped by being able to use overseas facilities. Our Army can respond with far more dispatch to such situations as that in Lebanon by having advanced staging areas from which to operate.

Critics of the program point to instances of inefficiencies or examples of money being spent unwisely. I am afraid it is true that in any operation of this size and geographical scope, with the pressures of urgent political necessities with which one must deal in various parts of the world, such examples are very apt to exist. We are making a determined effort to reduce or eliminate them and the conscientious study of the problem made by your Subcommittee for Review of the Mutual Security Program is rendering a constructive service by helping us dig out examples of deficiencies. However, I think it would be a critical mistake to curtail the program because of isolated instances of waste and inefficiency representing a small percentage of the total. When a city finds shortcomings in a police force, one does not abolish the force; the city works to improve it and correct the deficiencies uncovered.

One of the things that has puzzled me since coming to Washington has been the difficulty we encounter in developing a broad understanding of the importance of the mutual security and the military assistance part of the program. When General Twining was asked by a Member of the Congress last spring whether he would recommend restoring all the dollars that had been cut from the mutual security program before consideration of any possible increase in the regular defense budget, he replied forcefully that he thought these dollars would better be spent in the defense of this Nation by putting them into mutual security. The individual chiefs of the military services later authorized the chairman to say that they unequivocally agreed with him. This, it seems to me, is impressive testimony.

For each dollar we have spent during 1950-58, the nations receiving military assistance from us have spent more than $5. In fact, the 1958 effort was at a rate of $7 for every dollar of military assistance received. These countries are spending this for their own defense, of course; but this defense effort is also supporting our objectives as the leading nation of the free world. It is hard to see how we can possibly get better value for our dollar than by helping these nations stand on their own feet and carry their part of the load.

The record of achievement thus far is one that more than justifies rededication to the principles of military assistance and collective security. All over the world, at points of greatest potential danger, the fighting forces of our partner nations stand ready to take the brunt of initial attack on any scale and to hold the line until reinforcements can be rushed in to restrain and drive back the aggressor. This international cooperation has, in less than a decade, created a common defense posture in the free world which has successfully checkmated Sino-Soviet aggression and maintained the difficult peace which still prevails. Speaking as one primarily concerned with making certain that our defense is strong enough to meet whatever tests it may face, I strongly urge support of a program which contributes so much to our own national security at so moderate a cost, and which joins the forces of the free world in an effective military alliance committed to the preservation of the peace

NEED FOR A SHIFT
IN EMPHASIS*

CHESTER BOWLES

CHESTER BOWLES, *former United States Ambassador to India and presently United States Congressman from Connecticut, is the author of numerous articles on United States foreign policy.*

. . . At present most of our foreign economic aid is military aid. Even our nonmilitary aid largely concentrates on supporting the military programs.

The segment set aside for pure economic aid, moreover, concentrates too narrowly on measurable material development. It fails to recognize that such growth, however valuable, is only a partial answer to the problems now facing the less-developed countries.

Let us briefly examine the breakdown in last year's mutual security legislation. Total foreign-aid appropriations were $3.3 billion. Of this $1.5 billion, or about 50 percent, went straight for military aid.

The second largest sum, $750 million, went for defense support. This is the name we now give to extra aid for countries receiving military aid, extra aid to help their economies support the cost of an enlarged Defense Establishment.

Such economic aid, in other words, is not officially designed for economic development purposes at all, although it obviously may assist such efforts inadvertently.

Special assistance accounted for $200 million and the contingency fund for another $155 million. While grants under these accounts have been given for economic development, the general categories cover odds and ends of purposes that cannot really be classified in advance as earmarked for either military or economic development aid.

This left mighty little for straight economic development and technical assistance—only $400 million for the Development Loan Fund and $171.5 million for technical cooperation.

Thus we see that less than $600 million, or only 18 percent of

* An excerpt from "A Fresh Look at Foreign Aid" by Chester Bowles, *U. S. Congressional Record,* 86th Session, 1st Session, 1959, pp. 3479-3481.

more than $3.3 billion, was provided expressly and directly to help raise living standards and foster orderly political growth through technical cooperation and economic development. Even allowing for the economic development aspects of other programs, our mutual security effort, as it is conceived today, still remains largely a military aid program.

It follows that the administration and the Congress apparently still consider the major threats in Asia, Africa, and Latin America to be military threats, and that the principal danger against which we are attempting to insure ourselves in these areas is the danger of overt Sino-Soviet military aggression.

The hard facts do not support this assumption.

Vietnam, Korea, and Taiwan, to be sure, face the clear danger of invasion from Communist China or its satellites. Turkey, Greece, and Yugoslavia remain essential to the NATO defense line. All these nations will continue to need military assistance.

But the primary problems facing most countries of Africa, Southeast Asia, the Middle East and the Far East are not military problems.

Their problems are mainly concerned with the laying of the foundations for orderly political government. They are problems of national development in the broadest sense of the words.

In my opinion, our emphasis on military spending in such areas represents in large degree a waste of public funds. In some cases it feeds the disruptive internal forces which represent the principal threat to national security....

Furthermore, I believe that Congress and the public should be given a more realistic picture of what our aid program has accomplished and what it has failed to accomplish.

TIME IS RUNNING OUT

However, the weaknesses of some of our country-by-country programs are not my primary subject for tonight.

What concerns me most is our continuing failure to understand, much less to cope with, the revolution of rising expectations which is now sweeping the non-Western World....

People that have always accepted their poverty and hunger as unavoidable are now convinced that they can have a better life and have it soon.

They have observed that with industrialization come wealth, power, prestige, and security. So they also want to see their countries industrialized—soon.

As we have seen, the crucial question which ought to draw together the less developed countries, Europe and the United States is whether this economic and national development will take place under totalitarianism ór under governments based on the consent of the people.

The inauguration of foreign aid programs by the Sino-Soviet bloc in 1954 is tangible proof that they recognize what is at stake. The question is, Do we recognize what is at stake?

Communist extremists persuasively promise the underdeveloped nations a quick ride up the escalator to economic development. Just look, they say, what is happening in China.

Soviet aid in Asia, Africa, and Latin America is already pushing the $2 billion mark. It may be expected to double and then to triple in the next 5 years.

Unless the non-Communist governments of the less developed countries are able to meet the demands for agricultural and industrial developments by the methods of freedom and consensus, they will almost certainly be replaced by governments which are prepared to follow China's example.

ECONOMIC PROGRESS NOT ENOUGH

I have said that economic development is by no means the complete answer to the problems facing the less developed countries today. If there is to be orderly political growth, economic development must be accompanied by educational, social, and political changes which gives people an exciting new sense of participation and of increasing justice.

If these factors are missing, economic development may actually increase the disruptive tensions within the country by opening up expectations that cannot be met. It will almost certainly increase the explosive gap between rich and poor.

The problem of the less developed countries is to build themselves into viable nations. This is a tall order at any time. It is made doubly difficult today because these new lands are caught in the strong conflicting currents of world politics.

What are the essential requirements for a viable nation?

Most important of all, its people must develop a personal stake in the survival of the national government. They must come to believe that the state can help protect and promote their interests and that they will receive justice at its hands. . . .

When freedom comes, the exciting days of marching, singing crowds and of single-minded opposition to the colonial aggressor quickly fade into history. New governments are faced with the sobering and infinitely greater task of rallying their people in support of constructive programs that will kindle in their countries the desire to grow and endure as free nations.

What is the proper role for the United States in this difficult process?

We must understand the many-sided nature of the problem. Then we must tailor our economic efforts clearly to meet the broad category of problems that are encountered on the way to nationhood.

These needs include raising the level of literacy. An educated people can more easily be persuaded to support a responsible government while doors are opened to enrichment of individual lives.

They include land reform measures so that a higher percentage of the land will be efficiently used for food production and more individual farmers may have the satisfaction of owning their own property.

They include the development of a free, responsible labor movement.

They include programs of community development projects in the rural areas to help increase food products, control disease, build roads and schools, and create small village industries.

They include transmitting insights into modern public administration so that the new governments will be able to operate effectively with due respect for public freedom.

If our efforts are to succeed, we must recognize that Secretary Marshall was wholly right when he said that in working toward these objectives the initiative must come from the people and governments of the countries we are seeking to help.

Although we cannot force these developments, we can stand ready to help intelligently and seriously when our help is requested.

All too often we tend to think of all the less developed countries as one vast frustrating blur. This obscures the vital differences in importance, needs, and capacity for growth. . . .

Our own specially created democratic process is not necessarily or automatically the best model for an Asian or African country that lacks our historical background. The essence of democracy underscores the need for each people to create its own pattern of social, economic, and political life within the guidelines of its own heritage. . . .

Among the less developed nations themselves, these differences go far beyond physical and social forms. Almost all of the less developed countries stand in need of economic development before they can be viable, modern nations. But it is foolish to expect them to be equally able to absorb United States development help.

Why is it that a dam can be built and operated with great success in one country, while in another country a similar dam is a miserable failure?

Why is it that modern equipment can make a vital contribution to increasing agricultural and small industrial productivity in some countries while similar machinery, sent to other countries, lies rusting on the docks?

In most cases it reflects basic differences between the countries and the governments in question—differences which our program planners and our legislators have lamentably failed to take into account.

The underdeveloped countries fall into many categories. The most favorable opportunities for American assistance exist in those countries which are not only determined to build the economic and social foundations . . . but which also have the built-in capacity to implement their plans.

In such countries, which unhappily are altogether too few, we should be prepared to make bold, long-term investments of our capital and our skills.

At the other extreme are those nations which because of lack of farsighted leadership or of administrative ability, or both, are clearly incapable at this stage of meeting the minimum practical requirements of meaningful economic development.

Long-term loans or grants for the general economic development of such countries are foolhardy. Efforts to force the pace beyond their capacity to use the funds effectively will almost certainly fail, and failure will lead to frustration on our part and bitterness on theirs.

Between these extremes there are many variations. Although a particular country may not be ready for a long-term investment commitment, it may nevertheless be making an honest effort. This and the local political situation may combine to warrant a program of modest encouragement with the assurance of more substantial help as the administrative performance improves.

India is clearly the outstanding example of a country in the first category, where maximum aid can be used for maximum benefit. Moreover, India also serves to illustrate the standards by which I believe we should measure the capacity of each country to use our long-term economic development assistance.

FIVE STANDARDS FOR JUDGMENT

1. *The most important standard is the standard of self-sacrifice.* To become eligible for substantial long-term assistance, a nation should demonstrate as India has demonstrated that it is making a substantial effort to finance its own national development.

Evidence of this willingness for self-sacrifice includes a reasonably effective program of national taxation, controls over the importation of luxuries and nonessentials, and a determined and continuing effort to provide the maximum number of peasant families with their own land.

2. *A country's political importance also must be taken into account.* This may be measured by its population, the size of its territory, and its location. India again is the best illustration.

With her 400 million people, her strategic geographical location and her democratic institutions India is not just another underdeveloped country. It is a continent comparable in size, population, and potential influence to Europe.

Moreover, India alone rivals China in Asia. Although each is rushing forward to develop its resources, each is following a totally different path: India has chosen to follow the path of maximum freedom; China, the path of totalitarianism.

If the Indian democratic experiment fails, most Asians will be convinced that, like it or not, the Communist approach to economic development must be accepted as the only effective way.

3. *To qualify for major investment assistance, an underdeveloped nation should have put together a practical, comprehensive plan of objectives and itemized the allocation of resources necessary.*

Only in this way can the important tasks be given priority, the development program related to private and public income, and the need for international help judged more accurately.

If there is already a significant private business sector, it should be considered side by side in such a plan with Government-sponsored agricultural, power, and transportation projects in formulating a national development scheme.

India is now in the midst of her second 5 year development plan. It includes both private [and public] investment. . . .

4. *A qualifying country should have substantial number of able civil servants.* Without good technicians, honest tax collectors, and experienced administrators, large amounts of investment capital cannot be used to economic advantage.

One of the great residual advantages of British rule in India is the excellence of today's Indian civil service. We ought not to treat it as a wasting asset.

5. *In order to qualify for long-term investment assistance, a country should have a relatively stable government with popular roots.* As the largest democracy on earth, India obviously qualifies to a special degree. We should not, however, stretch this point to bar long-term assistance to all non-democratic governments.

As I have suggested above, we cannot reasonably expect all underdeveloped nations to develop in a democratic image to the degree that India is now striving to do. The decisive point is the responsiveness of each government to the public interest. . . .

Measured against these five standards I have listed, India qualifies to a special degree for American economic aid. So do several other nations. On this basis they should be assured of our intensive long-term investment support for their economic development programs.

As other countries approach these criteria, they should receive more aid because more aid can then be put to effective use.

But countries which are clearly unable to meet minimum standards should tactfully be told that they cannot expect investment assistance from us until they have created their own internal basis for development.

This does not mean that we should turn our backs on them.

We can recommend to them the creation of a comprehensive economic development plan.

Directly and through United Nations agencies, we can help provide tax experts, survey engineering teams, and other technicians to help them to create a workable administrative base.

We can urge them to inaugurate land reforms and suggest expert advisers with experience in introducing these critically essential programs previously in other countries.

We can also help them to finance individual projects which are worthwhile in their own right; that are not dependent on the economy of the country as a whole, and that are clearly in the people's interest.

A new modern hospital in the national capital is a good example of such a project, or an expanded and improved university or agricultural experiment college.

I must, however, stress that no set of criteria can solve all the problems of allocating American economic assistance.

Occasionally some economic aid will be needed for straight political support purposes or to backstop military aid, or as an expedient rental fee for the use of a military base.

But let us separate such aid in our thinking and in our programming from our major effort of constructive development assistance.

Let us recognize it for what it is: an expedient and, we hope, temporary, by-product of the cold war.

This approach will enable us to avoid much of the waste that comes from trying to promote a broad-scale development program in a country that is not ready for it, and that is unwilling or unable to make a genuine and reasonably effective effort to help itself.

Some will suggest that the standards which I have proposed may be construed and resented by many friendly, unprepared nations as political interference.

Some resistance is inevitable. But I do not believe that it will be of serious proportions. Tactful American negotiators, supported by a firm congressional mandate, could convince most governments that these criteria are essential in their own long-range interest as well as in ours.

Indeed I believe that many of these governments will actually welcome such standards as a lever with which to persuade reactionary elements within their own countries to cease blocking constructive reforms.

VII

The Proper Means
of Foreign Aid:
Public or Private

About the Readings

*In the discussion of using foreign aid as a proper means
of accomplishing American foreign-policy goals, one of the most
searching debates is between those who believe that the most fruitful type of aid must be through the channels of private enterprise
and those who contend that the emphasis must be on governmental
aid to the vast majority of the countries requiring assistance.
Although there are few commentators at either extreme, many have
argued that the emphasis should be toward one or another of these
alternatives.*

*The article entitled "Foreign Economic Aid and the American
National Interest" presents the argument for emphasis on governmental assistance. On the other hand, Professor Milton Friedman,
in the second article, offers a provocative challenge to some of the
assumptions of the supporters of governmental aid. Are there any*

areas of agreement between the two articles? What role, if any, do they both assign to governmental aid? To private aid?

The third article, by Donald Malcolm, is written with tongue in cheek, but it may be as sensible as some suggestions that have emanated from more serious circles.

FOREIGN ECONOMIC AID AND THE AMERICAN NATIONAL INTEREST*

BY THE RESEARCH CENTER IN ECONOMIC DEVELOPMENT AND CULTURAL CHANGE OF THE UNIVERSITY OF CHICAGO

The Research Center in Economic Development and Cultural Change of the University of Chicago is organized to conduct research on the problems of economic development and foreign economic policy. The Research Center sponsors the periodical Economic Development and Cultural Change.

From what has been said [in a preceding section], it follows that economic assistance (as distinguished from military assistance) should be extended to all underdeveloped countries outside the direct Soviet sphere. This assistance should be independent of whether these countries are or are not in a military alliance with the United States and even of whether at a given moment the public speeches of some of the political leaders of an underdeveloped country are friendly or unfriendly to the United States. In other words, economic aid should not be an instrument of either rewarding our friends or a means of gaining political influence and approval

* Reprinted from "Foreign Economic Aid and the American National Interest," a report prepared by the Research Center in Economic Development and Cultural Change of the University of Chicago for The Special Committee to Study the Foreign Aid Program, *The Foreign Aid Program,* 85th Congress, 1st Session, 1957, pp. 233-238.

in certain countries. There is an open or thinly disguised suspicion in many countries that American aid is often used as a bribe. The more impartially economic aid is extended the less basis will there be in the long run to such a charge.

But the main reason for the general extending of economic aid is not the sentiment of others, or their beliefs and feelings about the United States. It can hardly be in the national interest of the United States to make a particular country (or its leaders) like us. The reason why economic aid should be given to all underdeveloped countries—except those within the Soviet orbit—is the similarity of overall conditions and of potential effects of economic development in all of them.

. . . In most underdeveloped countries the emergent middle class, and especially the educators, government officials, and intellectuals, are the motivating force in the push for economic advancement and the changing social relations. These social groups are inclined to see in communism, or other forms of totalitarianism, the only alternative to the existing order, and the only means to economic development. They are aware of the necessity for expanded capital accumulation and investment; indeed, they often exaggerate the need for capital by emphasizing heavy industry in their ideology of economic development. They are equally aware that the traditional social orders which are breaking down due to western influence, do not provide the necessary political, social, and cultural conditions for development. They know that Soviet Russia has been successful in accumulating enough capital and in bringing about social changes necessary to development. Either they are ignorant of the ruthless means by which this was achieved, or they excuse them as steps necessary in order to break out of the age-old vicious circle of poverty breeding poverty that is characteristic of so many underdeveloped areas. Often, these groups gain as allies the peasants, who seek land reform, and the emerging industrial working class.

But though many of these persons are not frankly antagonistic to communism, they are not committed to it and would turn from it if a nonviolent alternative of achieving the aims of economic development at approximately the same pace as that allegedly possible by totalitarian means were shown to them. Hence the strategic function of American economic aid in such a case would be to show these middle classes a third alternative between the semifeudal status quo and totalitarian revolution. It is meaningless to say that in giving aid there must be no "intervention in the internal affairs" of the aid-receiving country, for any aid necessarily affects these internal affairs. In some countries this difficulty of intervention is less severe, since there the power of the upper classes has already been weakened, so that aid can be directed to helping non-Communist groups committed to changing their social environment remain in power and to help steer them in nontotalitarian directions.

This internal social transformation is the crucial determinant of the future political development of the countries of Asia and Africa, and such a development appears the best guaranty of their future political independence and noncommitment to the Soviet orbit. If such a middle class imbued by an ideology of economic progress by nonviolent means could have been created in Egypt after the anti-Farouk revolution, the intelligentsia of that country, instead of indulging in pan-Arab "imperialism," might have been so deeply concerned with the solution of the country's internal economic problems that the glamor of enlargement of Egypt's sphere of influence would have paled in comparison.

HOW MUCH ECONOMIC AID SHOULD BE GIVEN?

The social development sketched earlier depends in large part not only on the conditions under which it is offered, but also on the total magnitude of the aid. Before entering into a discussion of this problem, a clear distinction must be drawn between economic aid for development and other forms of aid—for military purposes, disaster relief, or other aims. This distinction is not aided by the general confusion which exists in the United States in classifying different forms of aid. Although a relatively clear distinction is made between economic aid and military aid, the category of defense support contains elements of both. In what follows we will confine ourselves to discussing economic aid in the form of technical assistance, grants, and soft and hard loans for capital investment purposes, commodity deliveries which supplement the productive effort of an underdeveloped country, and other measures which directly or indirectly contribute to the raising of productive performance.

Given this description of economic aid, it may be said that a small aid program, like the present technical assistance and development assistance programs, more or less as a token of America's interest in the development of the poorer countries, would be useless.

For the achievement of a rapid rate of growth without resort to totalitarian methods implies a rapid rate of investment, but a slower rate of voluntary savings. Part of this gap between savings and investment needed for rapid development could be met by drastic changes in the tax laws and their administration in underdeveloped countries, especially if the taxes could be imposed so as to fall on those who invest their savings in socially unproductive ventures. Another part of the gap could be covered by emphasis on community projects and other comparatively low-cost investments, aided by technical assistance. Judging from the experience of India under the first 5-year plan, this would result in an increase in income per head of only about 2 percent per year—better than stagnation, but not sufficient for setting in motion a genuine process of self-sustained growth in the underdeveloped countries.

Thus, if economic aid with a long-term political objective is to be given at all, it must be on a scale that enables the recipient countries to use substantially more resources for development than they can save. Probably at present not more than about 9 or 10 percent of the incomes of most of the underdeveloped countries could be saved without resort to totalitarian methods of forced savings. The rate of investment needed for a more rapid rise of per capita income at a rate of 3 to 4 percent per year (assuming an average rate of increase of the population of 1.5 percent), would be from 14 to 16 percent of incomes as a minimum. Private foreign investment of the type most useful for aiding development probably would contribute only relatively little. Since the total income of the "underdeveloped" countries in Asia, the Near East, and Africa (excluding China and underdeveloped countries in Eastern Europe) was approximately $110 billion in 1955, the gap to be filled annually by foreign economic aid would amount to a minimum of $3 billion, allowing possibly for private investment of the type most useful for economic development of about $1 billion. Some of this aid would doubtless be supplied by some of the more highly developed countries of Europe, especially to those parts of Africa where they have special political interests. For this reason a smaller lower limit might be applicable for economic aid extended by the United States. A lower limit would also apply if not all underdeveloped countries outside the Iron Curtain were eligible for inclusion in the program. The size of the program would also depend on the ability of the aid-receiving countries to use capital for purposes of development. The amount of aid needed for any such integrated program of development would remain close to the lower limit in the early stages of the program, since the absorptive capacity of many underdeveloped countries for genuinely productive development projects must first be improved. But gradually, as technical assistance speeded up the training of increased numbers of skilled workers, managers, technicians, and others, an expansion in the rate of development could take place. This training program would soon provide also fairly full employment for the potentially discontented elements of the middle class. It would reach a peak level of perhaps $5 billion per year in about 10 or 15 years, and then decline, since as the people in the aid-receiving countries might save voluntarily from one-fifth to one-fourth of any increase in their incomes, their savings would eventually increase faster than their ability to absorb capital for development. Also, as the strength of the capitalist sector of the new middle class grew, the climate for private foreign investment would improve, a fact illustrated by Latin American events in recent years.

But all estimates of the amount of foreign aid necessary for a long-term economic development program which would be in the American national interest are extremely uncertain, owing to the many factors impinging upon the relationship between foreign aid and economic growth. The estimates provided in this section were intended not as hard and fast amounts, but only as illustrations of the rough order of magnitude of the amount of aid which might be required to achieve the objectives stated in this report. On the one hand, expenditures on foreign aid of a few hundred dollars per year would fall far short of the need, but, on the other hand, spending tens of billions of dollars would be wasteful and unnecessary from the viewpoint of national security of the United States.

WHAT KIND OF ECONOMIC AID SHOULD BE GRANTED?

In considering the kind of economic aid that should be granted, two general considerations have to be borne in mind. In the first place, we must not forget that the overall pattern of development of presently underdeveloped countries differs from that experienced in the past by the advanced countries, and especially by the United States, and, above all, that the role of government planning for economic growth is much more widely accepted today than was the case in the 19th century. Hence economic aid should not be made contingent upon its being applied primarily for the fostering of privately owned capital. It would be a serious mistake to assume that some form of democratic, labor-party style socialism is merely a watered-down brand of communism. In fact, . . . the intervention on a rather wide front by governments in underdeveloped countries appears to be necessary due to the existing low educational and social level of the mass of the population. This provides the emerging middle-class intellectuals with great importance in these countries, and enhances the overall role the government is destined to play, at least in the initial phase of economic development.

Thus economic aid programs may have to be adjusted to the government-sponsored and often socialistic or quasi-socialistic development plans of underdeveloped countries; and, although some features of these plans may be very different from those of a private enterprise economy, foreign aid programs may have to be developed so as to fall roughly in line with development plans of the governments of underdeveloped countries. This does not mean that economic aid may not be given also to strengthen private enterprise in underdeveloped countries; in fact, it may be expected that even fairly socialistically inclined governments in underdeveloped countries will not object to private capital formation and the exercise of private entrepreneurial initiative, provided that this initiative is not centered on projects with little or no expectation of social (as against private) benefit. Conditions in underdeveloped areas are not similar to those that prevailed in the presently developed countries during the 19th century. Some countries with exceptionally rich deposits of high-grade raw materials can offer sufficiently favorable prospects to foreign capital to offset all the political and other risks involved in investing in present-day underdeveloped countries. Even in these countries, it is difficult to transfer the modern productive methods of the foreign-controlled raw materials sector to the rest of the economy, although some attempts have been made, for example, in Venezuela, to tax these foreign companies to provide expanded public services needed to make more widespread economic dvelopment possible.

Efforts to encourage the increased flow of private capital have included partial tax exemption (in the case of investments in the Western Hemisphere), credits for taxes paid to foreign governments, the negotiation of treaties with underdeveloped areas concerning the safeguarding of the rights of investors, United States Government insurance (called guaranties) against expropriation, insurance against inability to convert profits back into dollars, and other measures. But all of these steps have failed to induce much additional foreign investment. Little use has been made of the guaranty fund, and only $50 million of guaranties had been taken up by 1954. This was to be expected, since none of the attempts to encourage private investment could strike at the root of the matter, which is the antagonistic attitude toward foreign investors of important nationalistic groups in some underdeveloped countries, the political insecurity in some areas, and the poor prospects of yield in many industries in many underdeveloped countries. These conditions are to a large extent the result, as well as a cause, of underdevelopment. The signing of treaties against expropriation is less important than the day-to-day policy of the underdeveloped country toward capitalists, domestic as well as foreign. In some countries, many basic industries are reserved to government or to local capitalists. Foreign companies, because of their general unpopularity, dare not disobey the local labor laws, which may be very advanced considering the stage of economic development, while local enterprises can ignore them. Land reforms that may be undertaken for reasons of political stability and to provide the incentives needed for economic development may incidentally reduce the prospects for foreign investment in plantation agriculture. Rates charged by private utilities are sometimes limited to levels which make investment unprofitable.

Sometimes proposals are made to devise new means of encouraging investment. These include complete tax exemption of returns from foreign investment, the negotiation of stricter investment treaties, technical assistance in ways of attracting capital, more thorough guaranties, and greater use of the International Finance Corporation (a revolving, semipublic fund, affiliated with the International Bank for Reconstruction and Development, investing in industrial equities rather than in loans). Only the last really strikes at the root of the problem, by encouraging the growth of local financial institutions in the underdeveloped countries themselves.

Tax exemption will do little to encourage private investment, because even after the taxes of both, the United States and the capital-importing countries, are paid, the return on foreign investments

is often higher than on domestic investment. Wh
investment is not the tax on profits, nor any threa
fiscation or inability to convert profits into dollars,
ous uninsurable risks of a bad "investment climate."

On the whole, private investment, apart from some exceeding
rich mineral or plantation products, play an increasing role in
countries which are well along the road to economic development.
These countries enjoy, in general, greater political stability and have
a more predictable and equitable system of taxation. Thus private
investment is, in general, most willing to flow into those areas
where governmental inducements or guaranties are least needed.
Some of these considerations explain why American foreign investors have favored such politically safe and economically sound
areas as Canada, Latin America, and Western Europe as preferred
regions for placement.

The second problem toward which an economic aid program
should be directed is the promotion of economic development as its
central focus. Since . . . the main problems of economic advancement
in underdeveloped countries consist in the development of more
highly qualified personnel, more and better suited resources, and
a greater quantity of productive capital, economic aid programs
should feature prominently the creation of these three factors for
development. This will require that in the administration of
economic aid programs constant attention is paid to the long-run
potentialities of economic growth of the aid-receiving countries. It
also means that an economic aid program must be conceived as a
long-run enterprise and that some guaranty of its duration is as important as is the total magnitude of the program. For, as was
pointed out repeatedly in this report, the process of economic development takes time, and the execution of an effective development plan requires a fairly high degree of assurance that sufficient
funds will become available as the program unfolds in coming years.
Without such an assurance, some of the most basic programs of
creating various forms of overhead capital cannot be undertaken,
because the probability as to whether the supporting investments
can ever be made is too low. Thus, an important aspect of an
effective economic aid program is its being conceived as a long-
range program; i.e., a program which will continue on a sustained
magnitude over a period of 10 to 20 years, as a minimum.

One further point should be mentioned which affects the nature

.f the administration of an economic aid program. As is well known, the receipt of economic aid is regarded by many underdeveloped countries as a sign that they are not fully mature or equal; and in the face of old resentments against those who in the past have treated them as inferior, because they lacked political independence, the need to receive grants-in-aid is considered as a continuation of their status of political immaturity and deficiency. An aid program must be administered so as to minimize these sentiments of inferiority. We do not claim that Americans have shown an overbearing attitude in their behavior toward people in underdeveloped countries. On the contrary, we believe that the American matter-of-fact, let's-get-down-to-business attitude has compared favorably with the stiffer and more formal behavior patterns displayed by many Europeans or even Asians and Africans. The point we wish to stress is that in many underdeveloped countries, economic aid includes not merely the transfer of funds, technical assistance, and the like, but also the actual cooperation and advice in the working out of plans and programs of development. Not every underdeveloped country is in the position of India, which has technically competent people to work out a development plan, and whatever developmental planning is executed in some underdeveloped countries is sorely in need of improvement. It is in this field in which American expert advice and a proper administration of an economic aid program can bear considerable fruit. Yet, it should be recognized that it is a delicate matter to insist on improved plans for development without offending the sensitivities of officials and others in underdeveloped countries.

CONCLUSIONS

If a program of economic aid incorporating [these principles] can be adopted, it is fair to expect that it may result in a successful instrument of American foreign policy. Of course, there is no guaranty that matters will go as they have been sketched above, and the implementation of a sizable program of economic aid for development always will contain a noticeable factor of risk. However, in this it will not differ from any action taken in the field of foreign relations. Moreover, we have discussed here only a program of economic aid and this may and will be supplemented by a program of military assistance going to some of the same countries which are eligible for economic development aid. In the case of political developments which may endanger the success of the economic aid program, other measures, from military aid to actual forms of armed resistance to aggression, may have to be taken, if the situation demands. Thus a program of economic aid is neither a cure-all, nor will it create necessarily close friends among the underdeveloped countries. But if it can be successfully implemented, it is likely to lead to a stabilization in world political relations which should do much to reduce international tension and to improve the overall objectives of American foreign policy.

FOREIGN ECONOMIC AID:
MEANS AND OBJECTIVES*

MILTON FRIEDMAN

MILTON FRIEDMAN, *Professor of Economics at the University of Chicago, is author of numerous articles and books on a wide range of economic problems.*

. . . Two questions must be answered in judging government economic aid. First, is it likely in fact to promote the economic development of the countries to whom aid is granted? Second, do its political effects in those countries promote democracy and freedom?

The second question, though not much discussed, is easy to answer and admits of little dispute. As it has so far been administered, our aid program has consisted predominantly of grants or loans or provision of personnel or material directly to the governments of recipient countries for specified projects regarded as contributing to economic development. It has thereby tended to strengthen the role of the government sector in general economic activity relative to the private sector. Yet democracy and freedom have never been

* Reprinted from *The Yale Review*, Vol. XLVII (June 1958), 500-516. Copyright © 1958, Yale University Press.

either attained or maintained except in communities in which the bulk of economic activity is organized through private enterprise.

This problem has of course been recognized and partly explains why some grants or loans have been made to private enterprises in the recipient countries rather than directly to governments. Last year [1957], John B. Hollister, on the occasion of his retirement as head of the International Cooperation Administration, proposed that a much enlarged fraction of total funds be channeled to private enterprises. This modification, which aroused strong opposition and is not likely to be carried far, would reduce the tendency of the aid program to strengthen the government sector. It would, however, not eliminate it. We are hardly likely to make funds available to enterprises in poor standing with their governments or for projects opposed by governments. The final result will therefore be much the same.

Many proponents of foreign aid recognize that its long-run political effects are adverse to freedom and democracy. To some extent, they plead special extenuating circumstances. For example, the group in power in a particular country may for the time being be in a shaky political position, yet its overthrow may mean the assumption of power by anti-democratic forces. And economic aid may help such a government over its temporary political crisis. Their main reply, however, is that economic progress is a prerequisite to freedom and democracy in underdeveloped countries, and that economic aid will contribute to this outcome and thereby on balance promote political freedom. This makes the crucial question, even for political effects, the first, namely, the economic effects of economic aid.

The belief that foreign aid effectively promotes economic development rests in turn on three basic propositions: first, that the key to economic development is the availability of capital; second, that underdeveloped countries are too poor to provide the capital for themselves; third, that centralized and comprehensive economic planning and control by government is an essential requisite for economic development.

All three propositions are at best misleading half-truths. Additional capital is certainly essential for development. And of course the more capital the better, *other things being the same*. But the way in which capital is provided will affect other things. The Pharaohs raised enormous sums of capital to build the Pyramids;

this was capital formation on a grand scale; it certainly did not promote economic development in the fundamental sense of contributing to a self-sustaining growth in the standard of life of the Egyptian masses. Modern Egypt has under government auspices built a steel mill; this involves capital formation; but it is a drain on the economic resources of Egypt, not a contribution to economic strength, since the cost of making steel in Egypt is very much greater than the cost of buying it elsewhere; it is simply a modern equivalent of the Pyramids except that maintenance expenses are higher. Such modern monuments are by no means the exception; they are almost certain to be the rule when funds are made available directly or indirectly to governments that are inevitably under pressure to produce the symbols of modern industrialism. There is hardly an underdeveloped country that does not now waste its substance on the symbol of a government-owned or government-subsidized international airline. And there is hardly one that does not want its own steel mill as yet another potent symbol.

Some monuments are inevitable in the course of economic development and may indeed be politically desirable as tangible and dramatic signs of change. If the appetite for monuments were at once so intense as to make them the first claim on a country's resources and yet so limited and satiable that their extent was independent of the resources available, monument-building might be a costly fact of life but would have little relevance to foreign economic aid. Unfortunately, this is hardly the case. The appetite grows by what it feeds on. The availability of resources at little or no cost to the country in question inevitably stimulates monument-building. Thus while foreign aid grants may in the first instance add to the capital available to a country, they also lead to a notable increase in the amount of capital devoted to economically wasteful projects.

Cannot, it will be asked, these problems be solved by our exercising control over the use of the capital we make available to governments? And would they not be avoided even more directly if we adopted the proposal to make funds available directly to private enterprises? Aside from the political problems raised by any attempt at close control of even the funds we give, the answer is no. In the first place, there is a purely technical difficulty. Our grants are only part of the total capital available to a country and of the funds available to the government. It will do no good to control the use of the one part while exercising no control over the other; the effect would simply be to alter the bookkeeping—whatever we regarded as appropriate projects would be treated as financed with our funds, and the monuments would be built with local funds. Effective control would thus require us to control the whole of the capital investment of the country, a result that is hardly feasible on political grounds. But even if it were, the problem would by no means be solved. We would simply be substituting one central planning group for another. This leads to the third proposition: that central planning by government is essential to economic development. . . .

Let us turn now to the proposition that economic development requires centralized governmental control and planning, that it requires a coordinated "development program." This proposition, too, contains an element of truth. Government certainly has an important role to play in the process of development. It must provide a stable legal framework; it must provide law and order, security to person and property. Beyond this, it has an important role in promoting certain basic services, such as elementary education, roads and a monetary system; it can make an important contribution by extension activities which help to spread knowledge of new and improved techniques. And numerous other activities of the same sort come to mind.

But none of these activities calls for a centralized program for economic development or detailed control of investment. And such a centralized program is likely to be a hindrance, not a help. Economic development is a process of changing old ways of doing things, of venturing into the unknown. It requires a maximum of flexibility, of possibility for experimentation. No one can predict in advance what will turn out to be the most effective use of a nation's productive resources. Yet the essence of a centralized program of economic development is that it introduces rigidity and inflexibility. It involves a central decision about what activities to undertake, and the use of central force and authority to enforce conformity with that decision.

It may well be that in many underdeveloped countries, existing or potential government officials are as competent both to judge what lines of activity will be profitable and to run particular plants as existing or potential private businessmen. There is yet a crucial advantage in letting private business do as much as possible. Private individuals risk their own funds and thus have a much stronger incentive to choose wisely and well. They can be more numerous and they have much detailed information about specific situations that cannot possibly be available to governmental officials. Even more important, however wisely the decisions are made, there are bound to be mistakes. Progress requires that these be recognized, that unsuccessful ventures be abandoned. There is at least some chance that unsuccessful private ventures will be allowed to fail. There is almost none that public ones will be—unless the failure is as flagrant as the British ground nuts venture. The mistake will simply be concealed by subsidy or tariff protection or prohibition of competition. If anything is clear from widespread experience with governmental economic activity, it is that a governmental venture, once established, is seldom abandoned. And surely it is almost as clear that governmental officials are less experimental, less flexible, less adaptive, than private individuals risking their own funds.

What is required in the underdeveloped countries is the release of the energies of millions of able, active, and vigorous people who have been chained by ignorance, custom, and tradition. Such people exist in every underdeveloped country. If it seems otherwise, it is because we tend to seek them in our own image in "big business" on the Western model rather than in the villages and on the farms and in the shops and bazaars that line the streets of the crowded cities of many a poor country. These people require only a favorable environment to transform the face of their countries. Instead there is real danger that the inherited set of cultural and social restraints will simply be replaced by an equally far-reaching imposed set of political and economic controls, that one strait jacket will be substituted for another. What is required is rather an atmosphere of freedom, of maximum opportunity for individuals to experiment, and of incentive for them to do so in an environment in which there are objective tests of success and failure—in short, a vigorous, free capitalistic market.

Thus central control would be a poor way to promote economic development even if the central authorities chose individual projects as wisely as private individuals and with the same end in view. In fact, as we have already seen, the government is almost sure to promote other ends—the national and personal prestige that can be attained through monument-building—so that the case against centralized control is even stronger.

The issues we have been discussing are strikingly illustrated in a report submitted in December 1956 by the M.I.T. Center for International Studies to the Special Senate Committee to study the Foreign Aid Program. The report studies the problem of how to judge whether a country should be given additional aid. The answer is that the criterion should be whether the country is making an "additional national effort" toward economic development. Two, and only two, "rules of thumb" are given for deciding whether this is the case: "one index that national effort is being mobilized for development is the launching of measures to capture a good fraction of increases in income for the purpose of further investment"; another "measure of national effort . . . is the degree to which a country's leaders have worked out an overall development program."

Here are two of the basic propositions we started with. And the striking thing is that by these tests, the United States would never have qualified as a country making an "additional national effort" toward economic development! We have never had explicit "measures to capture a good fraction of increases in income for the purpose of further investment." Nor have our "leaders" ever "worked out an overall development program." And what is true of the United States is true of every other free nation that has achieved economic development. The only possible exceptions are the economic programs worked out after the Second World War by Britain and some other European countries, and these were largely abandoned because they were failures.

The only countries that satisfy the tests suggested by the M.I.T. report are the Communist countries—these all have measures "to capture a good fraction of increases in income for the purpose of further investment" and all have an "overall development program." And none of these has in fact achieved economic development in the sense of a self-sustaining rise in the standard of living of the ordinary man. In the satellite countries, the standard of living of the ordinary man has quite clearly fallen. Even in Russia, the ordinary man is by no means clearly better off now than before the Communists took over, and indeed, may be worse off even in terms solely of material comforts. While education and health services have clearly improved, food, shelter, and clothing have all apparently deteriorated for the masses. The achievements of which Russia justifiably boasts are to be found elsewhere: in its heavy industries, its military output, and its space satellites—achievements that from the point of view of the consumer classify strictly as monument building.

It thus seems clear that a free market without central planning has, at least to date, been not only the most effective route to economic development but the *only* effective route to a rising standard of life for the masses of the people. And it is eminently clear that it has been the only route consistent with political freedom and democracy. Yet the M.I.T. report and most other writings on the subject simply take the opposite for granted, without even noting that in doing so they are going against the whole of the evidence to date, and without offering a shred of evidence of their own. This is modern mythology with a vengeance.

What is involved here is no less than another phase of the ideological war in which we are engaged. A central premise of the Communist ideology is that the state must exercise comprehensive control and direction over the economic activities of its citizens; a central premise of Western liberalism is that free men operating in a free market can promote their own objectives without the necessity for an all-powerful state.

Foreign economic aid implicitly accepts this premise of the Communist ideology; yet it is intended as a weapon against Communism. Many who favor it as applied would be horrified at the idea of applying its principles at home. If they accept it, it is because they do not understand what it implies or because they take the word of the "experts" that it is the "only" way to win friends abroad. They, and the experts, are in the state of the man who discovered that he had been speaking prose all his life. Loyal Americans that they are, they have unthinkingly accepted a basic premise of the Communist ideology without recognizing it for what it is and in the face of the available evidence. This is a measure of the success of Marxist thought, which is most dangerous precisely when its products lose their labels.

Despite the intentions of foreign economic aid, its major effect, insofar as it has any effect at all, will be to speed the Communization of the underdeveloped world. It may, for a time, keep some of these countries nominally on our side. But neutral or even hostile democracies are less of a threat to the preservation of a free world than ostensibly friendly totalitarian countries.

An effective program to promote a free and prosperous world

must be based on our own ideology, not on the ideology we are fighting. What policy would be consistent with our ideology?

The aim should be to promote free markets throughout the world and maximum reliance by all countries on free enterprise in an environment favorable to competition and to individual initiative. We cannot do this by telling other governments what to do or by bribing them to go against their own natures any more than we can force men to be free. What we can do is to set an example and to help establish an international climate favorable to economic and political freedom; we can make it easier for other countries to take the path of freedom if they wish to.

The most important area in which we can do this is foreign trade. Here, in particular, our policies belie our professions. We profess to believe in free competition and free markets, yet we have erected barriers to "protect" domestic producers from competition; we profess to believe in minimal government interference with economic activity, yet our government imposes quotas on imports and dumps exports abroad because of a policy of government support of farm prices. True, we have also reduced tariffs and barriers to trade in many areas, and these actions, ably supplemented by the unintended effects of inflation, have reduced our trade restrictions to their lowest level in many decades. Yet those that remain, as well as the fresh restrictions that have been imposed, particularly on agricultural products, have, I believe, done far more harm to our foreign relations than any good we have done even temporarily by our economic aid. The rest of the world regards us as hypocrites, and they are at least partly right.

Entirely aside from the problem of foreign relations, these policies do us direct economic harm. They prevent us from using our resources as effectively as we might both at home and abroad; they hurt us as well as the rest of the world. A free trader like myself would like to see them abolished for this reason alone—in order to enable us to have a higher standard of living. But this is only part of the case for free trade, and, in the present context, the lesser part.

A major factor pushing underdeveloped countries in the direction of central planning and of autarchy is their lack of confidence in a market for their products. Suppose, they argue, we do follow the route of free enterprise and free trade, concentrate on producing those things we can produce most cheaply, and count on getting the goods we want to consume through international trade. Is not success likely simply to produce increases in import barriers by the United States and other countries so that we find ourselves all dressed up with a fine export industry and nowhere to go? And, under present circumstances, can one say with any confidence that they are wrong? Ask the Swiss watchmakers and English bicycle producers.

It is not often recognized how widespread are the implications of the restrictions on trade and, in particular, the uncertainty about them. We do not, it will be said, offer a market for the potential products of most underdeveloped countries so that our trade barriers do not affect them. But this is clearly wrong. It is a major virtue of free international trade that it is multilateral not bilateral. Were we to import more from, say, Western Europe, Western Europe would be able to import more from still other countries, and so on in endless chain, so that our own greater exports might go to very different countries than those from whom we purchased products.

Or to take yet another facet of the problem—the effect on foreign investment. In part, such investment is stimulated by trade barriers: if India will not permit the import of complete cars, an automobile company may set up an assembly plant. But this investment is wasted from the point of view of world productivity: it is used simply to do in one country what could be done more efficiently elsewhere. Productive foreign investment is hindered by trade barriers, both directly and indirectly. It is hindered directly, because trade barriers distort the incentives to investment and also make it more difficult for the investor to receive the return on his investment in the currency he wants—a country can earn foreign currency to pay him only by exports. It is hindered indirectly because business and trade relations among nations are a major channel for the spread of information about investment opportunities and the establishment of contacts that make them possible. Commissions of V.I.P.'s assigned the task of finding "investment opportunities" are a poor substitute for the day-to-day contact of numerous individuals engaged in earning their daily living by selling goods and rendering services in a foreign country.

Or again, look for the sources of American influence on foreign attitudes and cultures and where will one find them? Not in the literature disseminated by USIS, useful though that may be, but in the activities of International Harvester, Caterpillar Tractor, Singer

Sewing Machine, Coca-Cola, Hollywood, and so on. Channels of trade are by all odds the most effective means of disseminating understanding and knowledge of the United States.

British maintenance of free trade—whatever it motives—was surely a major factor knitting the nineteenth-century world together and promoting the rapid and effective development of many then underdeveloped countries. And trade barriers, currency controls, and other economic restrictions are surely a major factor dividing the twentieth-century world and impeding the effective development of the currently underdeveloped countries.

Suppose we were to announce to the world that we committed ourselves to abolish all tariffs, quotas, and other restrictions on trade by a specified date—say, in five or ten years—and that thereafter we would maintain complete free trade. Can there be any doubt that the effects on our international position—both immediately through the announcement effects and ultimately through the long-run economic effects—would be vastly more favorable than those achievable by any conceivable program of foreign economic aid even if one assigns to that aid all the virtues claimed by its proponents? We would be playing from our strength. We would be offering an opportunity to free men to make effective use of their freedom rather than contributing chains to enslave men.

It would, of course, be better if such action were taken by many nations. But it would be a serious mistake for us to link our action to that of others; the result would be to slow the movement toward free trade to the pace desired by the most recalcitrant member. Far better to move unilaterally. We would benefit economically and politically from a unilateral move, and we might have far more effect on other countries through example than over the conference table.

A movement toward free trade would affect adversely many particular individuals and concerns—those who have invested talent and capital in "protected" industries. But our mobility and adaptability are such that a gradual movement—over the course of, say, ten years—would give the affected individuals ample opportunity to adjust to the new circumstances with little if any loss. The new opportunities afforded by the expansion of world trade, and the more efficient use of our resources involved therein, would benefit many more than were harmed. After all, the transition to free trade over ten years would have far less of an impact than the technological changes that occur decade after decade and that we take in our stride.

As of the moment, we have a bear by the tail in our foreign economic policy—and unfortunately, it is not the Russian Bear. We get little if any political kudos for continuing economic aid—the recipient countries have come to take it for granted and even to regard it as their right. Yet for this very reason, the sudden cessation of aid would be regarded as an unfriendly and hostile act and would arouse great hostility toward the United States. Thus even if one accepts the arguments of the preceding sections, there remains the problem how to achieve the transition from our present policy to the alternative.

The simplest and least undesirable way seems to me to be to make a final terminal grant to each recipient country. The grant should be fairly generous, say something like two to three times the annual grants we have been making to the country. It should be completely unrestricted and preferably made in the form of a dollar—or even better a Swiss franc—balance on which the recipient country can draw as it wishes. In this way, our own involvement in central planning by other countries could be terminated at once, and the government of the recipient country would attach the greatest value to the grant.

The cost of such a termination program would be sizeable in the year of termination. But it would be a once-for-all cost rather than the steady and growing drain to which we appear to be on the verge of committing ourselves.

Foreign economic aid needs to be sharply distinguished from direct military aid and defense support even though it may be hard to classify any particular expenditure. Foreign economic aid consists of grants or loans from our government to other governments or to enterprises in other countries for specified projects regarded as contributing to economic development. It includes both technical assistance and grants or loans of money.

The objectives of foreign economic aid are commendable. The means are, however, inappropriate to the objectives. Foreign economic aid, far from contributing to rapid economic development along democratic lines, is likely to retard improvement in the well-being of the masses, to strengthen the government sector at the expense of the private sector, and to undermine democracy and freedom. The proponents of foreign aid have unwittingly accepted a basic premise of the Communist ideology that foreign aid is intended to combat. They have accepted the view that centralized and comprehensive economic planning and control by government is an essential requisite for economic development. This view is contradicted by our own experience and the experience of every other free country.

An effective program must be based on our own ideology, not on the ideology we are fighting. Such a program would call for eliminating the inconsistency between the free trade and free enterprise policies we preach and the protectionist and interventionist policy we at least partly practice. An effective and dramatic program would be to commit ourselves unilaterally to achieving complete free trade by a specified and not too distant date. This would do much to promote an environment and international climate favorable to the rapid development of the uncommitted world along free and democratic lines. It would be an act of truly enlightened self-interest.

AN EMINENTLY REASONABLE
SUGGESTION OF INCALCULABLE
BENEFIT TO THE NATION*

DONALD MALCOLM

DONALD MALCOLM *is a contributing editor of* The New Republic.

We were sitting at our desk the other day, and thinking of nothing special when, just like that, we discovered a way to end the recession and the Cold War at a single stroke. It seemed hard to believe at first, but subsequent examination of the idea has failed to turn up a flaw of any consequence. It merely requires, for its success, that the citizens of Russia accept, as gifts, all the automobiles this country can produce. And how can they refuse? If there is one impulse that the 20th Century has proved to be common to all mankind, it is the impulse to grip the wheel of a brand new car and sally

* Reprinted from *The New Republic,* Vol. 138 (June 16, 1958), p. 9. Copyright, 1958, by Harrison-Blaine, Inc.

forth, with manifold toots of the horn, in search of high adventure. We may take it, therefore, that the cooperation of the Russians is assured. Nor does it seem likely that our own State Department would enter a demurrer. What objection could there possibly be to such a brilliant stroke of diplomacy? As a peaceful and conciliatory gesture, it would be worth a whole Himalaya of Summit meetings.

Then who, we wonder, could object to a plan to provide every Russian with a free automobile? Certainly not the Pentagon, whose experts would be quick to realize that, in times of peace, the auto is a perfect weapon. By means of it, this nation might easily inflict upon its truculent international rival as much damage as it regularly inflicts upon itself, and this is no small thing. Every year in America, traffic accidents kill some 40,000 citizens, or the equivalent of three divisions, and injure about 130,000 others, or the equivalent of three army groups, while doing $5 billion worth of damage.

Perhaps it might bt argued that the automobile, despite recent substantial improvements, remains an inferior instrument of destruction as compared, say, to contemporary bombs. But surely this is to argue beside the point. Frightening as they are, these bombs cannot be used, for they must be held in reserve, as a deterrent to aggression. And there is this about deterrence: your opponent is none the worse for it. Deter him today and he will still be there tomorrow, requiring to be deterred again. But once a fellow has been run over, he has, so to speak, been permanently deterred. Thus, to continue testing explosives when we already possess, in the automobile, a weapon whose destructiveness we have thoroughly proved on ourselves is merely to sacrifice an assured result to a frivolous love of spectacle. For we must remember that no other weapon of comparable destructiveness can be used without arousing some degree of resentment on the part of its victims. Only the motor car has the skill to injure people without losing their good opinion.

But, you may ask, what of the ordinary American citizen, whose taxes must support this colossal enterprise? Well, *what* of him? During the present fiscal year, he has put up more than $40 billion toward a military establishment which, for all its awesome potential, has not achieved a stroke of useful work. Would he not feel better if he had something solid to show for all that money? After all, if a mere fraction of the military budget had been invested in automobiles for the Russians, the money would have earned, by this time, a really substantial return in the way of devastation and good will.

VIII

The Proper Means
of Foreign Aid:
Technical Assistance

About the Readings

Another problem of American foreign aid is the question of how much emphasis should be placed on strictly technical assistance efforts. There are varying opinions as to what role technical assistance can and should play in the American effort to utilize its economic capabilities to foster the sort of world that the United States wants to live in, but there are relatively few who completely oppose this aspect of the program. The argument generally comes over the extent of American involvement in this program. In the first article, Congressman Porter Hardy gives his analysis of the purposes of technical assistance; the second article, prepared by the Subcommittee on Technical Assistance, examines the question of whether or not greater emphasis should be placed on technical assistance activities at this time. Is there an intelligent line of argument that opposes the Subcommittee's view on the question of emphasis?

118

A CONGRESSMAN'S VIEW OF
TECHNICAL CO-OPERATION*

PORTER HARDY, JR.

PORTER HARDY, JR. *is presently a United States Congressman from Virginia and member of the Armed Services Committee of the House of Representatives.*

The objectives of this program are most inspiring and unselfish, particularly for an activity undertaken by one government on behalf of another. The technical co-operation program is founded in hope and optimism. It envisions a future in which, through the sharing of technical knowledge and skills, a better life can be created for millions of people in other lands—people for whom over the centuries tomorrow has always been bleak.

It is by no means accidental that the United States has led the way in this bold and imaginative undertaking. The stoic acceptance of life as it is has never been an American characteristic. We have always considered ourselves masters of our fate. Coupled with this confidence is a deep humanitarian urge which impels Americans into action whenever they see human misery caused by poverty, starvation, disease, and ignorance.

Moreover, when such conditions exist in lands with untapped resources, to an American it appears that what is needed is the application of American know-how to make the stubborn earth yield its stored abundance, to push back the ancient enemy of disease, to feed and clothe and house the people and give them the hope for tomorrow which seems so tragically lacking.

This is the central objective of the technical co-operation program. This is the valid element which finds a response in the heart of every American. This is why Congress so consistently supports this effort.

A praiseworthy objective, however, does not by itself assume success. Good intentions must be matched by wise actions. It is from

* Reprinted from *The Annals*, Vol. 323 (May 1959), pp. 18-21. Copyright, 1959, by the American Academy of Political and Social Science.

this standpoint that it becomes the duty of even the most ardent supporters of technical co-operation programs carefully and coolly to examine the nature of these activities and the way they are carried out.

Section 418(a) of the Act for International Development of 1950 defines technical co-operation programs as:

> . . . Programs for the international interchange of technical knowledge and skills designed to contribute to the balanced and integrated development of the economic resources and productive capacities of economically underdeveloped areas.

The United States contributes to this effort in three ways: by sending United States technicians to work in the host countries, by bringing host country personnel to the United States for training, and by contributing to the support of special joint bureaus set up within the host governments to carry out technical assistance programs. The emphasis throughout is intended to be upon the transfer of skills and know-how. Any expenditure for capital equipment is supposed to be limited to that needed for demonstration purposes only. It is, in other words, intended to be a program of education, not of economic aid.

The implications of this form of foreign aid are worth noting. One of the presuppositions of technical co-operation programs is that there are human and physical resources in the host country which will be employed as soon as the necessary know-how is made available. Another presupposition is that the host country can and will initiate, or take over and continue on its own, a given activity once the method of doing it has been adequately demonstrated. Finally, the concept presupposes that technical co-operation funds will not be employed to continue a given activity after know-how has been acquired by the host country. If additional United States dollars are necessary, they should either be provided through private sources or through other categories of the Mutual Security Program.

Out of a total of nearly 4 billion dollars of the President's budget request for the fiscal year 1959 mutual security program, 164 million dollars—about 4 per cent—was for technical co-operation. Thus the technical co-operation programs do not involve large sums of money when compared to the billions which we spend each year on other foreign aid activities. A portion of this amount represented United States contributions to technical co-operation programs carried out through international organizations like the United Nations and the Organization of American States. Of the total, however, 142 million dollars was for bilateral programs set up by agreement between the United States and individual host countries. The following comments relate principally to the bilateral programs.

I have already expressed myself as being impressed with the inspirational aspects of technical co-operation. It provides "people to people" contact—an element which should be supplied but is generally lacking in other aspects of our foreign aid program. Military assistance programs all over the world serve to protect the freedom of countries and their citizens—but the impact of such programs is not felt directly by the people. Military hardware does not fill empty stomachs. Economic assistance dollars too often are used for monumental projects such as dams and roads—projects which are primarily dedications to national pride. Although over a long period of time they contribute to an improved economy, they have little or no significance in the here and now for the ordinary man. The only programs that immediately encourage and directly help the individual are those embraced under the Point Four concept—that is, technical co-operation. Through these programs, individuals are helped to better health, to useful and enlightening education, to a more adequate diet, and to improved sanitation and housing.

In the current year over 3,000 American technicians are working abroad in some 50 countries. Most of these technicians are working with their counterparts overseas in the fields of food production, public health, and education. These are basic areas for the improvement of living standards. Some programs have been broadened, in response to changing needs, to help solve problems of transportation, housing, industrial management, public administration, and community development.

AGRICULTURE

In many countries technical co-operation programs have shown the way to better methods of cultivation, improved plant varieties and breeds of farm animals. Through these and the application of fertilizer to crops, improved tools and implements, control of plant diseases and insect pests, the production of food for hungry and growing populations has been vastly increased.

Even slightly improved tools or better methods of cultivation often make immediate and striking improvement. In Iran, a demonstration of the advantages of using a moldboard plow instead of a pointed stick in sugar beet cultivation resulted in three times the yield. In Ethiopia, a simple change to row planting of corn instead of broadcast planting increased production from 18 bushels an acre to 30 bushels.

Agricultural vocational schools and colleges have been opened in a dozen countries as a result of technical co-operation. Through agricultural extension activities, additional channels have been opened through which a continuous supply of scientific information flows to the farmers themselves in a form which they can understand and apply.

HEALTH AND EDUCATION

The original activity of technical co-operation in Venezuela was in malaria control. In three years, malaria dropped from third place to sixth among causes of death. In the Philippines, malaria incidence fell 68 per cent as a result of DDT spraying. The malaria control program, in addition to its striking accomplishments toward better health, had the important side effect of tremendous expansion in food production—particularly in Indonesia and Iran. Mosquito control restored to cultivation much highly productive land which previously had been abondoned because of malaria.

The surge of interest in education in all newly developing countries is a phenomenon of the present era. In 1946-47 in Cambodia there were 38,000 children in primary schools; in 1955-56 attendance was 241,000. In Iran, since the United States technical co-operation program began in that country, school enrollment has increased from 20,000 in 1948 to 45,000 in 1955. The great need everywhere is for trained teachers, and technical co-operation projects in education have concentrated on filling this need, helping to give pre-service training to more than 17,000 teachers and in-service training to more than 46,000.

I have given only a few examples to illustrate the operation of this program and the benefits it has produced.

Let us consider in more detail another example of accomplishment, in order to discuss the criteria applicable to a technical co-operation activity. In Chile, the government had sought over many years to establish a satisfactory program of preventive medicine. As part of the United States technical co-operation program in the field of health, during the period from 1943 to 1953, five health centers were established and operated in strategic locations. These centers have since been turned over to the Chilean government, which continues to operate them today. More important, using these original centers as a pattern, the Chilean government has constructed ten additional health centers in Santiago Province alone and has made such centers the basic field unit in a reorganization of the Chilean National Health Service.

All the elements of a successful technical co-operation project were present in this case: (1) The project dealt with a problem which had been of concern to the host government; (2) it involved a demonstration of method of solving the problem; (3) it resulted not only in an activity which could be and was turned over to the host government, but it stimulated expanded and continuing action by the host government in this particular field.

We have, as a matter of United States policy, sought to insure the presence of these elements by stipulating three conditions to be met in carrying out a technical co-operation activity. First, the host country must request it. Second, the host country must pay a fair share of its cost. Third, it must be related to efforts being made by the host country itself. . . .

GREATER EMPHASIS ON
TECHNICAL ASSISTANCE*

THE SUBCOMMITTEE ON
TECHNICAL ASSISTANCE

The Subcommittee on Technical Assistance of the Senate Foreign Relations Committee conducted an exhaustive survey of the purposes and results of American foreign-aid programs during 1956.

The subcommittee recommends that authorization of appropriations for technical assistance be stabilized at approximately the current level. It emphasizes that this recommendation is directed to technical assistance (the international interchange of technical knowledge and skills) and is not to be construed as applying to economic assistance and defense support.

The following shows the trend of authorizations and appropriations for bilateral technical assistance programs: in 1953 $189.8 million was authorized and $138.9 million was appropriated; in 1954 $140.2 million was authorized and $105.0 million was appropriated; in 1955 $117.1 million was authorized and $105 million was appropriated; in 1956 $146.5 million was authorized and $127.5 million was appropriated.

On the basis of its field observations, the subcommittee is doubtful that substantial additional funds could be administered effectively by the United States or absorbed efficiently by recipient countries.

The availability of American technicians to operate the program is a limiting factor which is too frequently ignored in proposals to expand technical assistance. Further, even if technicians and administrators were available, it would to some extent be counterproductive to increase substantially the numbers of Americans in certain countries.

The subcommittee has seen numerous examples of waste which arise primarily, it believes, from (1) poor planning, (2) inadequate

* Reprinted from U.S. Senate, Committee on Foreign Relations, *Final Report on Technical Assistance*, Report No. 139, 85th Congress, 1st Session, 1957, pp. 26-27, 43-44.

administrative follow-up, (3) the furnishing of more assistance than the local economy can absorb, and (4) an effort to produce impressive results in a hurry.

In Vietnam, equipment was supplied to a radio school and to a marine navigation school, but most of the graduates remained unemployed because of a lack of opportunities in the Vietnamese economy.

In Pakistan, equipment was supplied to a tuberculosis hospital, but the hospital staff did not know how to use it.

Also in Pakistan, insecticides which were supplied under a plant-protection program were allowed to remain on the docks until they deteriorated because the Pakistanis did not know how to use them.

In Thailand, some of the equipment supplied for a mechanic's school was more elaborate and complicated than graduates of the school would ever be called upon to use.

In Egypt, a demonstration health center was more lavish than Egypt could expect to afford for itself. In a case like this one, there is a danger that technical assistance may inspire unfulfillable desires, which may take the form of frustration and resentment of the United States.

It is because of considerations of this kind that the subcommittee is constrained not to recommend an increase in technical assistance. On the other hand, there are also many examples of successful, well-planned, prudently administered technical assistance projects.

The joint Commission on Rural Reconstruction in Formosa has been markedly successful in helping to raise the standard of living of Taiwanese farmers. A particularly noteworthy feature of its activities has been the introduction of improved breeds of hogs and inoculations against hog cholera.

The agricultural and community development programs in India deserve a share of the credit for fulfillment of the agricultural goals of the Indian first 5-year-plan. The community development program in particular is resulting in changing, more democratic attitudes between villagers and Government officials.

The village aids projects in Pakistan and the village development work of the Near East Foundation in Iran (financed in part by ICA funds) are also making significant contributions to the development of these two countries and to the achievement of United States goals.

In Vietnam, the tilapia fish project promises, at small cost to the United States, to result in a considerable improvement in the Vietnamese diet and in a stronger economic base for Vietnamese farmers.

And the American people can be proud of the contribution their government has made to malaria control in India and to bilharzia control in Egypt.

The subcommittee feels that with better planning, examples of this kind can be multiplied and examples of waste can be eliminated. It cannot be too strongly emphasized nor too often reiterated that technical assistance is a long-range program in which continuity of effort is at least as important as magnitude of effort. A basic project can hardly be well started in a year, much less completed in that time. The subcommittee has seen projects operated by private agencies which turned out to be highly successful, but which had to be carried on for as long as 6 or 7 years before they began to take hold.

It requires a rather high order of faith to persevere in projects of this nature when tangible results are not forthcoming immediately. This increases the importance of careful advance planning, rigorous screening of projects, and careful selection of supplies and equipment for demonstration purposes.

Results of the kind which the United States is seeking depend in large measure upon the readiness and willingness of the recipient country to make the most effective use of technical assistance. Where this situation exists in the recipient country, technical assistance is well worth the cost to the United States and the subcommittee would be disposed to look with favor upon sound proposals for increases in the program. But where this situation does not exist, it cannot be induced by unilateral efforts on the part of the United States. The proper course in such circumstances is simply to wait until the country is ready. In the meantime, modest programs with limited objectives may be justified.

In conclusion, technical assistance on a government-to-government basis is still a relatively new concept. Outside Latin America, the oldest country program has been under way scarcely 5 years. This is a brief period in which to launch and evaluate a long-range effort with as many implications as technical assistance. It has, in addition, been an extremely unsettled period with wars and threats of wars dominating the international scene and upsetting many otherwise well-laid plans for economic development.

In these circumstances, it is perhaps only natural that the technical assistance program has not produced all the results of which it is potentially capable. Some of the money which the United States has invested in technical assistance over the last 5 years has been wasted; but this should not obscure the fact that most of the money has produced results in the national interest of the United States.

The American national interest is the only valid test of a foreign policy. There has occasionally been some reluctance to apply this test in direct and specific terms to technical assistance. This reluctance stems, in part, from a feeling that such application lends credence to Communist propaganda that American aid programs of whatever kind are tools of imperialism designed to impose American dictates on newly independent countries. This reluctance is self-defeating in two respects.

First, it induces skepticism of our real motives on the part of underdeveloped countries. The people of these countries are not prepared to believe that we are wholly altruistic. When we are not perfectly frank about our real motives, they are more likely to give credence to the Communist version.

Second, this reluctance results in lack of understanding among the American people themselves. This accounts in part for the opposition to technical assistance and other forms of foreign aid as giveaway programs.

There is no reason for the United States to be at all hesitant about justifying the technical assistance program on the basis of its real motivation: namely the national interest. Far from imposing American imperialism on underdeveloped countries, as the Communists allege, the American national interest is in fact anti-imperialistic. Attempts to use the technical assistance program as an instrument of imperialism would produce the precise opposite of the results sought.

In many respects the national interests of the United States and of the underdeveloped countries coincide. So long as these countries retain freedom, independence, and economic growth as their national goals, the achievement of those goals is in our interest as well as theirs. This is the sense in which technical assistance is a mutual, cooperative undertaking promoting the enlightened self-interest of all concerned.

Although some mistakes and some false starts have been made in the technical assistance program in the last 5 years, there has also been progress in learning from the mistakes and in identifying the problems involved in a program of this character. In a number of countries, the technical assistance program has taken root. It would be a grievous error if, because of past mistakes, these roots were now destroyed. If the program is given sensible administration and if it is properly related to the overall objectives of our foreign policy, it can be reasonably expected to produce more results in the future than it has in the past. This is so not only because we can learn from past mistakes but also because the results of technical assistance are cumulative.

The concept of technical assistance is sound. Despite some waste, the investment which the United States has made in the program is also sound. The results to date justify further investment; indeed, the dividends from the investment already made will not be fully realized unless the program is continued.

IX

American Aid:
Two Case Studies

About the Readings

Although the discussion of American foreign aid has not yet been exhausted (nor is it likely to be), many of the most significant issues and viewpoints have been examined. There remains one very important area that deserves intensive consideration: the question of the proper way to administer the aid. Should it be administered primarily by personnel from the recipient countries or should the aid be channeled through an international organization in which the voice of the United States is not so loud? This debate is likely to become more intense in the future, but for the moment (summer 1959) it has subsided. It might be useful for the reader to develop arguments for and against a proposal to internationalize the administration of aid, and he may find that these arguments in many respects resemble those of the "experts."

Before the reader begins that project, however, he should read and study the two "case studies" that follow. One, Laos, is the enfant terrible of American aid experience, and the other, India, indicates some of the real accomplishments of the program. Are there any lessons to be gained from the two experiences?

LIVING IT UP IN LAOS*

IGOR OGANESOFF

IGOR OGANESOFF *is a foreign correspondent for the* Wall Street Journal *and a frequent commentator on American foreign-aid activities.*

A precedent of sorts has been set in this faraway Southeast Asian kingdom—free-handed Uncle Sam has suddenly snapped his wallet shut and won't pay out another cent of foreign aid until the Laotians promise to reform their currency.

Such undisguised interference in the internal affairs of a sovereign nation is uncommon in the annals of U.S. foreign aiders, who have paid out $60 billion to foreign governments since World War II. But the circumstances that prompted it are even more striking. They add up to a story of flagrant misuse of U.S. aid funds—and profiteering that may give Communist propagandists a weapon for upsetting the anti-Communist influence the aid program was designed to have in Laos.

Laos has been ecstatically drowning in American aid ever since 1955, not long after it was carved out of what used to be Indo-China. The nation was created as part of the settlement of France's war with Communist guerrilla forces for control of that former French colony.

ELEPHANTS AND AID

Often called "The Land of a Million Elephants," the country for the past two years at least, could just as well have been described as "The Land of a Hundred Million Dollars"—for that is roughly the amount the U.S. has poured into the local economy. For comparison's sake, the Laotian government's own income, mostly from custom duties, is barely $1 million a year.

Most of the U.S. dollars have been turned over directly to the Laotian government, either for various U.S.-sponsored economic projects or to support the 25,000-man Royal Laotian army. Strangely

* Reprinted from *The Wall Street Journal,* Pacific Coast Edition (April 9, 1958), p. 1. Copyright, 1958, by Dow-Jones & Co., Inc.

enough, the Minister of Plans, who administers the whole program, as recently as last fall was battling the army as leader of a Communist guerrilla force that kept fighting after the main Indo-China truce. He joined the government under terms of a cease-fire. The peculiarities surrounding the U.S. aid program here, however, are too widespread and have gone on too long to be attributed solely to this gentleman.

Local traders buy America's aid dollars from the Laotian government, purchase goods abroad and sell them for kip (the native currency) in Laos. These imported goods—supposedly—are of a nature to raise the Laos standard of living and to provide working tools for industrial expansion.

The principal effect of the U.S. largesse, however, has been a wild and rather weird boom, based on nothing more solid than cash on hand and an unquestioned assumption that there is more to come.

FORDS AND FEATHER DUSTERS

Sleek Cadillacs, Buicks and Fords have been imported by the dozen, although the principal highways still are hardly more than jungle trails. Other items on last year's import list make delightfully wacky reading—four and a half tons of feather dusters, 73 tons of sporting goods, fishing tackle and thermos jugs, 180 tons of automobile covers, $13,400 worth of festival decorations, $11,500 worth of musical instruments, and thousands of dollars worth of costume jewelry.

Retail shops are stocked to their bamboo ceilings with items that the Laotians have hardly ever seen before—American toothpaste, badminton racquets, roller skates, Japanese dolls and French perfume.

A lot of U.S. money went to buy products from Red China—cherries in syrup from Shantung and Five Goats beer from Canton. Much of this stuff is unsalable, but it doesn't matter; the importers have already made their profits from foreign exchange manipulations.

THE MAGIC KIP

To understand this, one must acquaint himself with the magic kip, the highly overvalued Laotian currency unit. The official exchange rate, set by the Laos government, is 35 kip to the American dollar. But in the hard-headed money markets of Hong Kong, Bangkok or even in Vientiane, a Laos trader can buy 100 kip for a dollar. This sets the stage for fantastic profits.

A Laotian trader can buy 100,000 kip in the free money market for $1,000. He then applies for an import license for, say $1,000 worth of building cement, but puts up only 35,000 kip to get the $1,000 from the government at the official rate. This leaves him 65,000 kip before he has even moved the goods. Then he can simply sell his import license for more cash, if he wants.

If an importer decides to use his license, he still stands to profit heavily. Suppose he imports inexpensive men's shirts at $1 each. Buying his dollars from the Laotian government at the official rate, each shirt costs him 35 kip. But then the free market money values come into play. When the shirt goes on the market in Laos, it is priced at about 100 kip. So the importer has nearly tripled his money. Repeating this process under Laos' free and easy import rules, a businessman quickly can amass a considerable fortune.

REPORTS OF COLLUSION

In neighboring Bangkok, reports of collusion between foreign exporters, particularly in Hong Kong, and Laotian traders are commonplace. One source estimates that only about 20% of the contracts from Hong Kong are free of kickbacks to importers for underweight, underfilled or overpriced shipments, which allow the importer to further build up his foreign exchange hoard.

Many shipments, it is said, are diverted in Thailand (95% of Laos' imports pass through Bangkok and then are transported to Laos overland), where there is a lively demand for a wide range of goods. Other items arrive in Vientiane only to be shipped out again for greater profits. Thus, industry-less Laos has become an exporter of automobiles and outboard motors.

It is estimated, although no one really knows, that well over half of the goods paid for never reach the Laos market. "The country is now straining to absorb $12 million worth of goods, yet $35 million is supposed to be coming in. If all this stuff actually arrived, it would be lying all over the streets," claims Ralph A. Epstein, a management consultant with the American firm of Howell & Co., of Washington, D.C., which has sent a three-man mission here as part of a $2,576,000 U.S. aid project in civil administration.

AID BREAKDOWN

Since 1955, the United States has provided $15.8 million in assistance that was supposed to go for specific economic development projects. Another $31 million has been given in the form of salable commodities to generate needed local currency for these projects. And $30 million-or-so yearly has been to support the army.

Before the aid program can be resumed, the U.S. insists the Laos government must devalue its currency and enact other reforms in handling the aid funds.

Though there have been temporary suspensions of aid to other countries—Yugoslavia and Egypt—in the past, these were ordered because those nations shifted their foreign policies closer to Russia's, not because of dissatisfaction with their domestic economic doings. And in no case was any cut as drastic, in terms of the effect on the country's economy, as the action taken against this tiny jungle kingdom promises to be, if the suspension is not lifted soon.

Laotian officials, right up to the cabinet level, are fighting hard to prevent the proposed exchange revision. Many, like the Minister of Health who controls the Pharmacie de Laos, the largest drug house in the country, operate flourishing businesses which would be seriously affected by any change in the present rules of the game.

"If Laos ever enacted a conflict of interest law," snorts a local American official, "the country would have to give up either government or commerce. They couldn't do both."

In this new jungle nation, of course, it might be difficult to find people outside the business community qualified to fill government posts. Mr. Epstein, one of whose jobs is to school Laotians in the arts of government, attests to this difficulty: "You can't make ministers of trade out of elementary school graduates."

NO ONE SEEMS WORRIED

No one in Laos seems overly worried that the Americans will stand firm in their demand for currency reform. Both sides expect the deadlock will be broken before June [1958] when Laos' next budget must be drafted.

"What would happen here if American aid were withdrawn permanently?" Prince Souvanna Phouma, prime minster, and son of aged King Somdet Prachao Sisavang Vong, is asked.

"It seems so unlikely that we have not considered such a possibility," he replies blandly. "Laos is part of the Free World and I can hardly conceive for what reason the United States, the principal supporter of the Free World, would refuse us aid. Laos has done nothing to justify abandoning us."

The Minister of Plans is solicitous Prince Souphanouvong, another son of the king who until a cease-fire last year was leading a Communist guerrilla army against his father. Patiently, the prince emphasizes that the U.S. will lose favor with the population if it insists on the kip devaluation and continues to suspend aid.

What does he think about his role—administering an aid program designed to strengthen Laos against Communist attack and subversion? "If you offer something better than Communism, the people will take it," the Prince answers smoothly.

"A LONG RANGE PROGRAM"

"We want internal peace and neutrality in foreign affairs," he says. "Our people shouldn't be left or right. The U.S. aid program was badly administered in the past but we hope you will continue to help us. My ministry is now drafting a long range program for using American aid."

The talk around Vientiane is that Prince Souphanouvong may be getting ready to claim the credit for straightening out the U.S. aid program in Laos.

Even the local U.S. officials privately will admit doubts that they can ever achieve a complete reform in the aid program, even if the currency exchange reform goes through.

"There is still no assurance that Laos will import the things it really needs to improve the economy, rather than luxury goods," one International Cooperation Administration man admits.

I.C.A. officials, uneasy at the flood of unessential imports financed by the U.S., did win one major concession early this year. They were allowed to place a representative on Laos' National Export-Import Council, with the power to veto any import. The current I.C.A. man, L. G. Daniel, suffers from a major handicap, however, in pursuing his job as watchdog. All the Council's deliberations, and the import applications as well, are in French—a tongue Mr. Daniel neither speaks nor reads.

Besides the kip devaluation, the U.S. now wants to institute a monthly release of project funds with strict accounting by the Laos government on its uses. At present, funds for an entire project are released in a lump sum and the I.C.A. loses control of the money completely from that point. As a result, Laos officials, besides granting import licenses for luxury goods, often have siphoned off the funds for their own uses, some of the U.S. representatives claim.

There is a lush building boom going on. Leading traders and government officials (often the same people) are huddling with architects and contractors for lavish new residences or flashy additions to formerly modest homes. Both the Laovieng Bank and the Bank of Indochina are preparing to move into sleek new glass brick and concrete structures. The Finance Ministry is constructing an ultra-modern building right next door to the newly completed Ministry of Plans.

"CERTAIN FAVORS"

It is generally agreed that some two or three hundred leading families in Laos (population: 3,000,000) are getting most of the benefit from the massive import program. One I.C.A. official frankly admits that "certain favors" are granted Laos political and government leaders to keep them "friendly," but he declines to elaborate further.

Meanwhile, back in the countryside, the rank and file of the Laotians, a handsome dark people, live much as they have always lived, oblivious of the U.S. help. Their flimsy shacks are built on stilts to protect them from snakes and flooding during the rainy season. They farm rice and a few vegetables and raise chickens. In the torrid climate only the scantiest cotton clothing is needed and hardly anyone wears shoes.

The Communists, of course, don't hesitate here or elsewhere to exploit corruption in government or riches flowing to a few favored hands. And Americans here are beginning to wonder how long the United States, in doling out assistance, can afford to ignore this unfortunate part of their program.

Talk to I.C.A. officials and they will admit that, except for a few projects, their whole program to date hasn't gone far in raising the standard of living of the general population.

IMPRESSING THE LAOTIANS

"One trouble is that in 1955 we started to throw in anything just to impress the Laos government," says one official. "And now we're stuck with a bunch of assorted, unrelated projects but no real program. It would be easier to start all over again than to correct what we have."

However, Laly La Verne, newly named chief of I.C.A.'s mission in Laos, firmly upholds the value of the program. "Maybe not much has seeped down to the little guy," he says, "but I know one thing—without U.S. military aid, this country would be part of Communist North Vietnam, and that certainly wouldn't help the little Laotian."

Husky, crew-cut Colonel Quan Rathikoun, chief of staff of the Laos army, proudly insists he would still have an army without U.S. aid, "though it would be a little smaller."

U.S. officials remain skeptical. The U.S. has been paying for everything the army uses, from radio parts and training ammunition to fish, tea and rice provisions and all salaries, the total coming to about $1 million every two weeks.

Complicating the army picture is the fact that it is currently engaged in absorbing into its ranks 1,500 Pathet Lao (Free Laos) Communist soldiers, who had engaged in six years of deadlock war up until last November. Under the 1957 treaty agreement, their leader, Prince Souphanouvong, gave up the provinces of Sam Neua and Phong Saly, bordering Communist China and North Vietnam, in return for a voice in the Royal Laos government. The remaining 6,500 soldiers in Prince Souphanouvong's army are being discharged to go home, but are required to register in their villages and carry special identity cards.

CROSSING THE MEKONG

The strictly economic projects are equally beset with problems. One of the few visible results of the I.C.A.'s efforts is a $600,000 ferry system, crossing the mighty Mekong River separating Laos and Thailand. It was completed last September and the U.S. bore all the cost, including a 15-month training course and natty, khaki uniforms for the 37-man staff.

Unfortunately, at the moment operating costs are $4,000 a month and revenues are only $700 to $800. U. S. aid funds make up the difference. The reason for the deficit is not hard to find. Only a few yards from the nearly empty ferry, Chinese junks are loaded to the gunwales with crates, oil drums and passengers. The junks are owned by a Chinese businessman who was foresighted enough to obtain an exclusive transport contract with the Thai rail monopoly, Express Transport Organization, which carries nearly all the freight to and from the Laos border and the big market city of Bangkok.

Another big project is the Napandgy dam where 700 to 800 acres of new farmlands are being created. It's a two-hour jeep trip from Phonsavona, where you see native workers carefully scraping the pollen off poppies for cooking into thick opium paste.

Although the local U.S. experts are hopeful that Napandgy and other dam projects will eventually result in a balanced agriculture, with corn and other profitable crops, they are bucking a strong tradition. The Laos people, by nature and their belief in ascetic Buddhism, are not prone to help themselves very much or to strive for material betterment. Given fertilizer that will double his yield, the Laos farmer may simply halve his planted acreage. And if a family member dies, very likely his plot of ground is taken out of cultivation.

However, farm betterment programs are proceeding full tilt. Agricultural experiment stations have been set up, to improve strains of local rice so that it matures evenly, to introduce rust resistant coffee to rebuild what once was Laos' major export before World War II, and to improve local strains of poultry and livestock.

I.C.A. representatives still blush over the $27,000 tilapia project. Local ponds were stocked with these imported fish. Then it developed that while the local populace didn't like their taste, the other fish in the ponds did and quickly gobbled up the entire supply.

Now the I.C.A. is importing meaty Berkshire hogs, to cross them with the local sway-backed but very hardy Chinese hogs. Already some of the U.S. officials think a mistake is being made. One American agricultural expert has written in a report. "Local hogs are scavengers and it is questionable whether an improved breed can withstand the rigors of a country where even the subsistence level of the people is not very high." For poultry improvement, Rhode Island Reds and White Leghorns have been imported, although the local populace holds a superstitious prejudice against white chickens.

REHABILITATING ROADS

Transport improvement is the largest single current aid project, with $5.6 million provided by the United States. Besides the new ferry, there's a $3.7 million plan to rehabilitate roads. Most of this has been spent for heavy earthmoving equipment, tractors, bulldozers and shovels. Maintenance cost of this machinery is about seven million kip monthly, or more than double the Laotian government's normal total revenue—which gives some idea of the problems ahead if the U.S. aid funds are permanently terminated.

Actual road work is largely in the hands of the Universal Construction Co., an American firm which operates on a direct contract with the Laos government and has a large force of Okinawans on the job. The principal project is maintaining the dirt road between Vientiane and the summer capital of Luang Prabang, 150 miles to the north. No new roads are contemplated.

Funds also have been set aside for moving Vientiane airport from one side of town to the other. The present site, it is claimed, is subject to flooding (though I.C.A. officials admit there is no concrete evidence of this) and not suitable for expansion because of adjoining rice fields.

Just under $600,000 has been provided for industrial development. A small part of this has gone into mining, mineral and power surveys but the bulk has been paid for three diesel electric generators totaling 2,200 kilowatt capacity, which are to be installed in Vientiane. The generators have been here, unused, since last June [1957] but there's no high tension wire around for transmission lines. The units are for temporary use until it is decided whether to put in permanent hydroelectric or steam power plants in the area. Continuous operation of the generators, all year round, will cost the Laos government $200,000, or a fifth of its normal income—another indication of the long-lasting nature of Laos' dependence on U.S. aid.

AID AND THE INDIAN
EXPERIMENT*

BY THE INTERNATIONAL COOPERATION
ADMINISTRATION

DEVELOPMENT PROGRAMS

India's Five Year Plans encompass almost every phase of agricultural, industrial and commercial life and also set goals for progress in education, health and social welfare. It was estimated early in 1956 that perhaps 87 percent of the First Five-Year Plan's goals would be reached. Agriculture, particularly production of food grains, took high priority in the First Five Year Plan; industrial development receives larger weight in the Second.

The targets set for food grain production in the First Five Year Plan had already been reached by March 1955, with an increase of 11.59 million tons. Whereas India had to import 4.7 million tons of cereals in 1951, this figure had dropped to 808 thousand tons in 1954, resulting in large savings in foreign exchange. A greater agricultural production will continue to be of primary importance—both in order to raise the very low levels of consumption and to keep up with a numerically large population increase.

Industrial production also moved ahead. The index of industrial production rose 22 percent between 1951 and 1955.

A total outlay for the first Five Year Plan was expected to be about $4.2 billion and for the Second Plan more than double this amount—about $10.08 billion.

By far the greater part of Five Year Plan expenditures has been financed out of India's own resources. Foreign assistance includes World Bank loans, aid from the Colombo Plan nations, from the Ford Foundation and other sources and U.S. bilateral assistance. Exclusive of the $190 million wheat loan, which preceded the present Indo-American program. U.S. assistance, on an authorization basis, amounted to about $330 million as of June 30, 1956. Colombo Plan assistance from Australia, Canada, New Zealand and the United Kingdom under the First Five Year Plan amounted to about

* Reprinted from *ICA Country Progress: India,* ICA: Washington, D.C. (November 1956).

$100 million. World Bank loans to India amount to nearly $125 million but $42 million was utilized before the Plan period. Of the balance available during the Plan period, $58 million was in the form of loans for private firms and $25 million was for the public segment of the Plan. Ford Foundation assistance has been about $11 million. Norway is assisting a fisheries project in southern India, at a cost of about half a million dollars.

Under the Colombo Plan, Australia and Canada have aided power development and transportation projects and Canada is supplying an atomic reactor to India. New Zealand has aided the All-India Medical Institute and dairy development projects. The United Kingdom has provided equipment for technical institutes. Ford Foundation activities have been largely in the training of men and women, at all levels of education, for rural development work although the Foundation is now doing a good deal of work in the small industries field.

The Soviet Union has agreed to build a steel mill in central India, on a loan basis, to cost the equivalent of $100 million.

U.S. ASSISTANCE

The present bilateral program of development assistance and technical cooperation dates from the general agreement between the United States and India of January 5, 1952. The agreement was set to run five years.

This agreement affirmed the desire of the governments of India and the United States "to cooperate in . . . accelerating the integrated development of India"; their conviction that "increase in the interchange between the two countries of technical knowledge, skills, and techniques in the field of economic development is mutually advantageous"; the recognition that "individual liberty, free institutions and independence on the one hand, and sound economic conditions and stable international relationships on the other hand, are mutually interdependent."

Some technical cooperation had been instituted before 1952 and the United States also had extended the $190 million wheat loan in 1950, in a period of emergency. Out of the assistance of $330 million during 1952-56, a total of $82.5 million was in loans (fiscal 1955 and 1956 programs). The balance of $247.50 million represented grants for economic development and technical assistance.

On August 29, 1956, a $360 million agreement was signed for the sale of U.S. agricultural commodities to India over a period of three years. India will pay for the commodities in rupees and the equivalent of $234 million in rupees will be loaned in India for economic development. The equivalent of an additional $54 million will be an outright grant to India, also for economic development. Other rupee proceeds will be used by the U.S. for costs of the diplomatic mission in India and for U.S. purchases of Indian products. The U.S. commodities to be sold include wheat, cotton, tobacco, rice and dairy products.

Each cooperative activity under the Indo-American program is embodied in a project agreement or a supplement to such an agreement. The project agreements now number about 60.

From the beginning, these projects have been selected through consultation of members of the ICA Mission in New Delhi and the members of the Planning Commission of the Government of India. Projects proposed by the Planning Commission are all in the context of India's Five Year Plans. In many cases, such proposals will have already been preceded by a great deal of study and analysis by the Planning Commission before being presented and in many cases specific plans have been worked out. The two primary tests are the acceptablility of the proposal under U.S. legislation and high priority of the proposal in Indian development plans. Broad fields of activity are these:

AGRICULTURE AND NATURAL RESOURCES

The major program in agriculture have been designed to increase agricultural production as quickly as possible and at the beginning of the present program in 1952, first agreements provided for import of fertilizer, import of iron and steel for farm tools and implements and a program for drilling 2000 large irrigation wells to supply water. Although India's gains in food production under the First Five Year Plan may be attributed to a variety of factors—including favorable climatic conditions, more land under cultivation and more land irrigated—activities of the Indo-American program made an important contribution.

Nearly 150,000 tons of steel have been supplied for use in agriculture. More than 215,000 tons of fertilizer were sent to India in 1952 and 1953. Use of ammonium sulphate fertilizer has more than doubled as Indian farmers have learned to increase crop production by this means. India's Sindri fertilizer plant has been producing at capacity and expansion of its facilities is under way. Additional fertilizer plants also are being planned.

The original irrigation program for 2000 "tubewells" was expanded eventually to 3000 wells, each capable of irrigating 300 to 400 acres of land. The first 2000 wells have already been drilled and subsequent programs are nearing completion. Exploratory drilling has been initiated to discover groundwater resources in 13 areas. One such exploration is now complete and operation under way in the remainder.

Additional activities in agriculture cover a wide range—plant protection and locust control, determination of soil fertility and fertilizer use, modern storage of food grains, agricultural and home science extension and training. Allied with these projects are expansion and modernization of marine and inland fisheries, development of forest research and desert afforestation.

INDUSTRY, MINING AND POWER DEVELOPMENT

Import of steel for industrial uses and for railroads has been the largest program of this nature. A large part of rupee proceeds from sale of steel in India, the equivalent of about $15 million, has been loaned to the newly organized Industrial Credit and Investment Corporation which the World Bank and private sources are also assisting. This corporation makes available credits to private industry for expansion of plants and other development purposes.

U.S. industrial engineers and consultants assist Indian industrial concerns in increasing production by working along with management in industrial plants. The industries aided range from steel mills to plants making machine tools and consumer goods. The work of an American foundry specialist resulted in the establishment by the industry of a foundrymen's institute, where advanced techniques are taught to foremen. Assistance also has been given through eight management associations.

U.S. aid also is being used to buy equipment to help India complete several major river valley development projects, each of which will materially assist in irrigation and in supply of electric power for industrial uses. Three of these are the Hirakud development in the State of Orissa in eastern India, the Rihand project in

Uttar Pradesh in northern India and Chambal project in Rajasthan and Madhya Pradesh in north central India.

The 14-mile long Hirakud dam will create the fourth largest man-made lake in the world, will provide irrigation for 2 million acres and produce 123,000 K.W. of electricity. Hirakud began storing water in July 1956. The Rihand project is just getting under way. It will permit irrigation of 450,000 acres by canal waters and will furnish electricity to operate tubewells irrigating a 1.6 million acre area. Rihand will generate 300,000 K.W. of electricity. The Chambal project includes three dams, a diversion dam, 255 miles of canal and will provide irrigation for 1.4 million acres, as well as 60,000 K.W. of electricity. Other projects being assisted are the Mahi, Ghataprabha, Kakrapar, Tapti Valley, Gangapur and Tunga Anicut.

Technical cooperation funds also have been used for engineering services to the Damodar Valley Corporation, a multi-purpose project patterned after TVA in the United States. Several units of the Damodar project are already in operation, others under construction. India is financing the development from its own resources, plus a World Bank loan.

TRANSPORTATION

India's dependence on its railway system is great. In the first three years of the First Five Year Plan, the Government of India placed orders for 769 new locomotives to be paid for from its own resources. The U.S. is assisting railway rehabilitation with 100 additional locomotives and 8,730 freight cars. The 100 locomotives and 6800 of the freight cars have already arrived in India and the remaining freight cars will be delivered by December, 1956. A team of 18 top American railway experts is currently making a survey of the operations of the Indian railways system. Their study will include recommendations on the coordination of rail-sea coastal traffic, the short-term measures needed to relieve the pressure on the rail system and the capital expenditures to expand the system and meet the demands created by the Second Five Year Plan.

Another cooperative project has to do with expansion of aviation ground facilities. Since India has an important location on round-the-world air routes and is served by two major American air lines, among others, improvements are of international significance.

LABOR

In the labor field, cooperative projects include establishment of the Central Labor Institute, as well as a study of the effect of temperature conditions on industrial workers and a project for trades training.

HEALTH AND SANITATION

The major effort in health is the nationwide malaria control program, aimed at reducing the annual number of cases from perhaps 80 million a year to a small fraction of this number, thereby permitting a surveillance program to be maintained at a fairly nominal cost. Studies also have been made of the feasibility of complete eradication of the disease. The nationwide control program involves cooperation of central and state governments, with U.S. support consisting mainly of crews and supplies, and miscellaneous items for use in research. Extensive operations in 1954 and 1955 have already reduced the estimated number of cases from 80 million to 40 million.

Another important joint project is the national water supply and sanitation program, intended to demonstrate methods of sanitation in all parts of the nation, particularly in smaller cities and rural areas since the larger cities have modern water supply and sanitation systems. The Government of India expects, during the course of the Second Five Year Plan, to expand this program greatly through activity by local communities themselves.

EDUCATION

Projects in education, under the Indo-American program, include assistance to technical education institutions and home science education and research. American universities working in cooperation with similar institutions in India include the University of Illinois, University of Wisconsin, University of Tennessee, Kansas State College, Ohio State University and Rensselaer Polytechnic Institute.

COMMUNITY DEVELOPMENT

India's community development program, often referred to as a "silent revolution," is making history. Inaugurated on October 2,

1952, anniversary of the birth of the late Mohandas K. Gandhi, father of Indian independence, this program of all-round rural development is already affecting the lives of more than 80 million rural people.

The initial Community Projects program, for intensive development, has been supplemented by the National Extension Service, for less intensive work, and the two have been integrated into a nationwide system bringing improved techniques and knowledge of health, education, agriculture and small industry to the villages.

Primarily an effort to stimulate self-help and cooperation in village life, the community development program has shown impressive tangible results, such as reclamation of 895,000 acres of land, irrigation of 1.5 million more acres, establishment of 12,000 new schools and 30,000 adult education centers, building of 28,000 miles of new road, including 3300 miles of hard surface road.

United States assistance to the community development program has been in the form of jeeps and other transport equipment for project officers and workers, agricultural implements to be used in demonstrations, health laboratory equipment, motion picture projectors and other teaching aids. In the training centers where village workers and project officers are instructed, American agricultural extension specialists and other technicians have performed a useful task in developing study courses and conducting demonstrations.

Prime Minister Nehru's evaluation of the importance of the community development program was given in the community development magazine *Kurukshetra* in October, 1955. Mr. Nehru said:

"I think that we may modestly claim to have achieved a great deal in many fields of human endeavor during these past years in India. But I believe that the most significant development in India has been this development of Community Projects and National Extension Service in the vast rural areas of India. For the first time, it may be said with truth, that we tackled the rural problem in a realistic way."

U.S. TECHNICIANS AND INDIAN PARTICIPANTS

As of May 31, 1956, 137 American technical specialists were assigned to India. These include 60 in agriculture and natural resources development, 28 in industry, mining and labor, 28 in education, 10 in community development, 11 in health, sanitation and social welfare. A total of 401 Indian participants in the program had studied in the United States and returned home; 54 were still in this country. Of these, largest numbers were specialists in agriculture and natural resources, industry and mining, health and sanitation.

COMMENT FROM INDIA

"In volume of total assistance to other nations much of it gratuitous and more involving resources which could easily have been absorbed in unprecedented domestic expansion, the U.S. example will be very difficult to emulate, let alone surpass."—*Statesman,* Jan. 7, 1956

"The simple ceremony at which the American Ambassador turned over to the Indian Railways the first four of the 100 locomotives which are being given by the U.S.A. should serve to remind one of the common ideals and mutual goodwill that bind the two countries. . . . The remarkable feature of U.S. assistance is that not only does the Administration provide help in accordance with official policy but the American people and private organizations like the Ford Foundation have contributed in a variety of ways to supplement India's own efforts in the fields of health, education and community development. Such goodwill is the result of the deeper cultural affinities which in the past made the U.S. a fervent advocate of Indian freedom and which can be trusted to prevail over differences in approach to passing issues."—*Indian Express,* Jan. 5, 1956

"There can be no more powerful factor in cementing friendly world relations than cultural and economic cooperation. It has, however, its dangers which have to be guarded against. If it leads to economic dependence in the sense that the country's progress depends too much upon foreign aid, it will not only be a source of demoralization but weakness. No progressive country which wants to build up its strength and independence can put itself in that position."—*Hindustan Times,* Jan. 5, 1956

"There are many in this country who recognize the post-war U.S. aid program as one of the finest and most sustained acts of generosity that the world has witnessed in modern times."—*Times of India,* Oct. 14, 1954

Selected Readings

BINGHAM, JONATHAN, *Shirt-Sleeve Diplomacy: Point-4 in Action,* New York: John Day, 1954. A readable account of the "essential factors regarding the purpose, organization, operation, and needs of the point IV program."

CASTLE, EUGENE W., *Billions, Blunders & Baloney: The Fantastic Story of How Uncle Sam Is Squandering Your Money Overseas.* New York: Devin-Adair, 1955. Through interviews with "the man in the street all over the world" Eugene Castle concludes that American foreign-aid program has been "clouded with the blunders, wrong guesses, bad timing and gross extravagances of well-meaning but pathetically unqualified American policy makers and representatives."

Committee for Economic Development, *Economic Development Assistance,* New York: Committee for Economic Development, 1957. Advocates an improved, enlarged and long-term program of United States economic aid to free countries in order to improve the prospects for stability and independence in those areas now "dangerously unstable."

ELLSWORTH, P. T., *The International Economy,* rev. ed. New York: Macmillan, 1958. One of the best written textbooks on international economics.

GARDNER, RICHARD N., *New Directions in U.S. Foreign Economic Policy.* New York: Foreign Policy Association, Inc., January 20, 1959, (Headline Series #133). Results of past American economic aid and the changing world scene have made necessary an examination of new approaches in the U.S. foreign economic policy. These "new directions" are examined in the light of national objectives and the Communist economic offensive.

International Development Advisory Board, *A New Emphasis on Economic Development Abroad.* Washington, D.C.: International Development Advisory Board, 1957. A report to the President by the Eric Johnston committee on "ways, means and reasons" for United States aid to international economic development.

KRAUSE, W., *The International Economy*. Boston: Houghton Mifflin, 1955. An examination of problems and policies found in the world scene today; written for the general reader and not for those with more than an introductory knowledge of economics.

MYRDAL, GUNNAR, *An International Economy*. New York: Harper, 1956. An examination of the problems of achieving economic integration on a world scale; for example, the conflict between national and international integration which has been accentuated by the drive of the underdeveloped countries for independence.

NIXON, JUSTIN WROE, *Man's New Hope: A Religious Approach to Foreign Aid*. New York: Church Peace Union, 1957. Believes that foreign-aid programs to promote the less developed areas of the world are both in the national interest and in accord with the humanitarian and religious traditions of the American heritage.

OPLER, MORRIS E., *Social Aspects of Technical Assistance in Operation*. Paris: UNESCO, 1954. An examination of the relation of technical assistance to the broad social structure and cultural patterns of the recipient countries in terms of the planning and selection of projects, the administration and execution of projects and the qualifications of the expert personnel needed in technical assistance missions.

U.S. Senate, Special Committee to Study the Foreign Aid Program, *Foreign Aid Report*. Washington, D.C.: Government Printing Office, 1957. A compilation of the studies and surveys made by the committee pursuant to the American foreign-aid program.

VINER, JACOB, *International Economics*. Glencoe, Illinois: The Free Press, 1951. A comprehensive analysis by one of the more provocative thinkers on international economic affairs.

WIGGINS, JAMES W., and HELMUT SCHOECK, eds., *Foreign Aid Reexamined: A Critical Appraisal*. Washington, Public Affairs Press, 1958. Papers from a symposium on culture contact in underdeveloped countries at Emory University, Atlanta, Georgia (1957) written by behavioral and social scientists. Various views are expressed on the social consequences of politically inspired economic aid to the underdeveloped areas.